Cont

G000115748

In Wainwright's Footsteps

The Pennine Journey

A guidebook detailing a modern-day route for a circular walk in the Pennines, from Settle to Hadrian's Wall and back, first trodden by Alfred Wainwright in 1938

A. Walker

Published in 2016 by:CM&CK Cocks
Yolanda
Brewery Yard
Stroud
United Kingdom

email: aw@awalker.me.uk
website: awalker@me.uk

Designed & typeset by A Lambert
Cover design by iindie Ltd
Printed in the UK

ISBN print: 978-0-9956043-1-5
ISBN ebook: 978-0-9956043-2-2

British Library Cataloguing-in-Publication Data
A catalogue record for this book is available from the British Library

Dedication

To the map-makers and the people of the dales. Without their contributions there would be no guide.

Introduction

In 1938, many years before he became well known for his guidebooks and television appearances, Alfred Wainwright decided to forego his more usual visit to the Lake District and explore the Pennines instead. He, like many others, was concerned as to the turn that international affairs were taking vis-a-vis Adolf Hitler and his intentions regarding the future of Europe. Britain had begun to make noises about such a state of affairs not being good enough and was fast reversing into a corner from which there would be no diplomatic return.

In the shadow of this, he plotted a temporary escape in the form of a long walk in the Pennines and in September he set off from Settle. As he began his planning he had not set himself a target but, remembering his school days, he thought of Hadrian's Wall and how he would like to see its remains. So it was that his goal was determined and his battle lines were drawn as to how he would walk the 200 miles from Settle and back. Rather fancying himself as something of a writer, he wrote a story of his trek, which was finally published under the title A Pennine Journey after his popularity was established in 1986. His account was not prepared in the form of a guidebook and from it his route could only ever be estimated through some minor detective work. I was struck by the notion of retracing his steps sixty years on, so in September 1998, having completed the route preparation as best I could, I set about repeating his walk. Along the way I would note what had and had not changed and I would walk alone in order to place myself in the same shoes as the quiet man whose name had since become synonymous with lone-walking.

It was not my intention to consider a guidebook for the walk as I knew that much of Wainwright's route was along roads that, though they may have been quiet byways in 1938, would now be thundering arteries of a countryside overrun with traffic. I intended my journey as personal recreation although I too promised myself that I would write my own account for publication only if a company believed it to be of sufficient merit. In the event of it having been published then you will find it under the subtitle of 'Back to the Wall'. It was during my walk that I began to consider the feasibility of a new long-distance route that was circular in form and visited many places of interest en route. It would not do to recommend Wainwright's route without revision, for to follow it with our modern-day traffic levels would be tantamount to lunacy. However, with some minor changes, the main aspects of it could form the basis of a superb eleven-day expedition.

For my part, I wished to repeat the walk – for better or for worse – as closely as possible to that taken by Wainwright and only upon my return did I then commence the operation of finding alternative paths and tracks. Only when I had walked the full length would I know what was and was not acceptable. It seemed most fitting that I make use of a technology that could not even have been dreamed of in 1938. I would obtain 1" maps that were contemporaneous with Wainwright's journey and would scan them via computer and enlarge them so that their scale equated to the modern 1:25000 map series published by the Ordnance Survey. This would not only provide me with the basis for route identification but would provide interest in the knowledge that it was those same maps to which Wainwright had referred during his weeks of planning.

How to use this guide

In assembling this guidebook I have taken one liberty, made various assumptions and have used the original 1" maps enlarged to the equivalent of the modern 1:25000 scale to lend authenticity to the route. They also provide for direct comparison between the old and the new. The one liberty that I have taken is in referring to Wainwright as AW – I have not done this to appear as though he and I were close friends but simply to avoid needless repetition of his full name.

The principal assumption is that to complete the walk will take eleven days; the same as originally undertaken by AW. The guide has, therefore, been prepared in eleven chapters, each representing one day's walking. I have made one or two changes to the route and have altered one overnight stopover to shorten an otherwise overly long and tiring day. These will become clear as the guide is followed. The old maps used are as follows:

Sheet No.		Revision	Days used
25	Ribblesdale	Second War (1940)	1, 11
20	Kirkby Lonsdale & Hawes	Second War (1940)	1, 2, 3, 10, 11
13	Kirkby Stephen & Appleby	Second War (1940)	3, 4, 8, 9, 10
14	Darlington	Second War (1940)	3, 4
10	Alston & Weardale	Second War (1940)	4, 5, 7, 8
6	Hexham	Second War (1940)	5, 6,

The fact that many things have changed in the intervening 60 years and also that the Ordnance Survey now show more detail on their 'Outdoor Leisure' series leads me to the assumption that in following the route you will do so supplemented with a modern map. Although it is entirely possible to follow the route from my description in conjunction with the scaled-up old maps, I believe that it is wisest, and will give more enjoyment, if you are armed with the route shown at the current 1:25000 scale. This will enable more accurate navigation and give reference points to highlight changes. The modern maps required are as follows:

Sheet No. Title	Revision	Days used
OL2 Yorkshire Dales (Southern & Western)	Outdoor Leisure	1, 10, 11
OL30 Yorkshire Dales (Northern & Central)	Outdoor Leisure	2, 3
OL31 North Pennines (Teesdale & Weardale)	Outdoor Leisure	3, 4, 7, 8
307 Consett & Derwent Reservoir	Explorer	4
OL43 Hadrian's Wall (Haltwhistle & Hexham)	Outdoor Leisure	4, 5, 6, 7
OL19 Howgill Fells (and Upper Eden Valley)	Outdoor Leisure	8, 9, 10

It is now possible to prepare custom maps that could be produced to minimise the number of maps to be carried. The OS website provides more detail.

The maps for each section of the walk show AW's original and my proposed routes as coloured dotted lines. I have deliberately prepared the route markings as subtly as possible as I wished to keep to a minimum my own amateurish artwork on these fine old maps. The routes are indicated as follows:

. . . . = Wainwright route

. . . . = Proposed route

Beyond these markings I have neither added nor removed any information from the 1940s' maps. They contain the same detail as AW would have had reference to in planning and undertaking his journey. There are a number of occasions where I have referred to a grid reference for route confirmation – these references are from the current National Grid and any grid referencing found on the scaled-up maps should be ignored.

The description of each day's walk relates more to the associated history of the places within each section – I conclude that the actual route-finding will present little difficulty in navigating the walk. This is, in essence, more of a guide to show where we have been rather than where we need to go.

It only remains to study this guide, decide as I did that you too would like to follow in the footsteps of Alfred Wainwright and then to plan and execute your own escapade. It may add further to the sense of fulfillment if you are accompanied by the account of his trek, A Pennine Journey and perhaps if I may be so bold, by my own account "Back to the Wall".

With our maps and books in hand we can set off together; I would be only too happy to walk all those miles again, for they were a fine liberation.

There is no inn at the end of the walk where you might claim a drink but if I hear of your adventure I might stand you a half. Good luck.

DAY NO.1

SETTLE TO BUCKDEN

DAY NO. 1

SETTLE TO BUCKDEN

T oday is an easy start to our journey with generally straightforward route finding. Divergences from AW's route are necessary to avoid unpleasantly
excessive road walking between Settle and Horton and again in upper Wharfedale. The day is split into five legs as follows:

Leg	From:	To:
1 – 1	Settle	Stainforth
1 – 2	Stainforth	Horton
1 – 3	Horton	Foxup Moor
1 – 4	Foxup Moor	Horse Head
1 – 5	Horse Head	Buckden

A total distance of approximately 19 miles takes us from Ribblesdale, over Foxup
Moor and into Littondale with a second, more testing ascent, before a gentle valley saunter
following the Dales Way to Buckden in Upper Wharfedale. Our route will also encounter
two other long distance paths; the first being the Ribble Way that we follow for some distance in the Ribble valley; the second being the Pennine Way that we will pick up as we
leave Horton via Horton Scar Lane.

Although there is little to delay progress, a stop at the Pen y Ghent café is almost educational, pausing awhile to see the antiquated clocking-in device used for those undertaking
the Three Peaks Walk. The pull-up out of Littondale is a long slog that saps the energy and
seems to take forever. It is best to allow eight hours for this first leg.

Two maps are required for the day from the 'Outdoor Leisure' series:

OL2   Yorkshire Dales (Southern & Western)

OL30   Yorkshire Dales (Northern & Central)

DAY NO. 1/MAP NO. 1 SETTLE – STAINFORTH

When AW left Settle, he did so by following what is now the B6479 and he took this path up the eastern side of the Ribble valley all the way to Horton in Ribblesdale. It would be foolhardy to directly retrace his steps as modern traffic levels render such a venture as both unpleasant and decidedly dangerous. There are no pavements beyond Langcliffe and the verges are uneven and not made for walkers. Even if they were smoother, they are not the place to savour a walk in the country.

So, we ignore AW for the first stretch and instead our route crosses the River Ribble on the B4680. Once across the bridge, just before the school grounds, we follow a narrow path abutting the school fields that runs more or less parallel with the river. The path here is part of the Ribble Way. The building on the east side of the Ribble noted as 'The Shed' was once part of the Langcliffe Mill complex involved in the spinning and weaving of cotton. It is now a retail outlet known as Watershed Mill.

Following the western side of the river, our route rises until it becomes close to but high above the river, opposite the buildings referred to on the map as Langcliffe Place Cotton Mill. The mill still employed some 250 workers when AW passed but, like so much of Britain's textile production, cotton manufacture ceased in the 1950s and it now operates as a paper mill. The mill's postal address is 'Christie's Mill', paying regard to Lorenzo Christie and his son Hector, the owners of the mills from 1861. Hector is commemorated in the village church, recognising his establishing of the Langcliffe Institute. The map's reference to Langcliffe Place is actually the rather more grand accommodation for the mill owners.

Crossing Stainforth Lane, we then walk parallel to the road for 200 yards, after which our way follows the gentle slope to the left of the trees. We then follow right down a winding track leading to the delightful hamlet of Stackhouse. The cottages here provided housing for the cotton mill workers.

Following a track signposted 'The Locks' (the locks referred to are the water race built upstream from the mill to provide power to the looms and which also incorporated a salmon leap), our route then follows the western bank of the river where, after a mile, a short detour takes in the spectacle of Stainforth Force. The River Ribble's waters are squeezed through the constricted valley and provide a tumultuous cascade, especially after a spell of rain.

Crossing the river and road into the village of Stainforth, modern visitors will not find the café that existed when AW was here and even the inn was closed on my last visit. I am afraid refreshment will have to wait until we reach Horton in Ribblesdale.

A little way beyond Stainforth Force we leave the Ribble Way and follow the minor road to the hamlet of Little Stainforth. We must turn onto the quiet road heading northwards and follow the quiet macadam road to Helwith Bridge. At the hotel, a track leads off northwards back on the Ribble Way, before passing under the Settle–Carlisle railway to then join the western bank of the river.

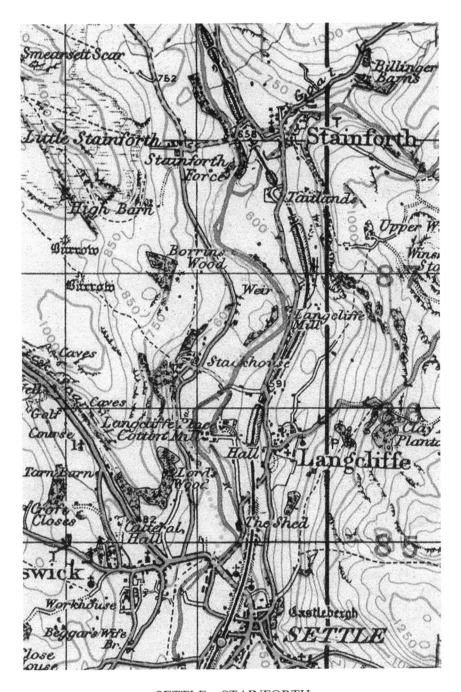

SETTLE – STAINFORTH

DAY NO. 1/MAP NO. 2 STAINFORTH – HORTON

Having borne witness to man's construction endeavours at Langcliffe, there is much evidence of his destructive powers hereabouts. The land to the west of the path has been decimated and the scars of quarrying detritus has wreaked havoc on any claim to beauty. Arcow quarry has changed the topography dramatically and reference to the new maps of the vicinity clearly show how the contours have changed in the intervening years as great chunks of the hills to the west have been devoured.

Arcow quarry is the first of many violations that have been meted out by man on his surroundings that we will witness. It is easy to think that such scars could only have been savaged by machine but back in the day such labours were largely undertaken by hand using mere manpower. One such man was Maurice Lambert who, when interviewed after his retirement, recalled his time at the local quarries of Foredale and Arcow.

He started work in 1944 at Foredale quarry in the role of breaking and filling, which entailed breaking limestone with a sledgehammer and loading the stones into rail-mounted trucks. These were then pushed to the top of an incline prior to their descent to the kilns, which would then produce powdered limestone. The empty truck was then returned to the rock face and the back-breaking work would continue.

Maurice Lambert left the quarry for two years' service in the forces in 1947 and returned to work at Arcow in 1949. Breaking and filling was still a role of hard labour, with the only mechanisation being the use of the trucks to shift the stone to the kilns. He outlined that, at that time, there were extensions to these rail tracks that would lead to the main line. Around 16 of these trucks would be filled each day and it is hard to imagine this output being produced day-in day-out.

He moved between various local quarries and each role was unimaginably physical. Even more extraordinary is the fact that he worked like this until his retirement, which came as late as 1990 when he was offered voluntary redundancy. AW could have considered himself lucky that the worst of this commercial vandalism only took place after his passing in 1938.

The track proceeds northwards, following close to the west bank of the river, until the road is reached near to the bridge over the Ribble in Horton in Ribblesdale. If you are looking to give up and return to Settle then the railway station is to the left, but our route follows to the right across the bridge. The reference on the map to New Inn refers to a hamlet rather than a third village hostelry and the bridge is known as New Inn Bridge. We follow the road south for a short distance to the Pen-y-ghent café, where it would be wise to rest awhile as the café is the last chance for refreshment before Buckden, still 11 hard miles distant.

Leaving the café, we proceed south for a few yards until a track leads off eastwards at 'The Old Vicarage' in the direction of the great bulk of Pen-y-ghent.

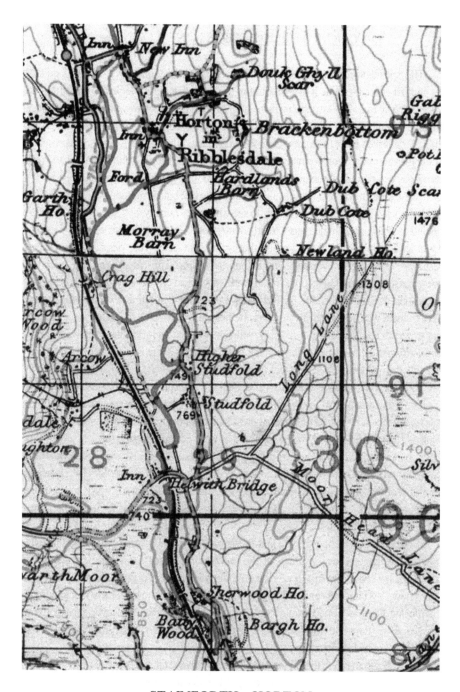

STAINFORTH – HORTON

DAY NO. 1/MAP NO. 3 HORTON – FOXUP MOOR

This splendid green track heads eastwards towards Pen-y-ghent and leads us quickly up and out of Ribblesdale. It is at the start of this track that our route finally joins the route taken by AW (and it is also at this point where the route coincides with what, years later, became part of the Pennine Way). Although slightly off route, it is worth a visit to Horton's church, dedicated to St Oswald, which has a complete Norman nave and is recognised as being the most complete Norman church in the Yorkshire Dales. Although AW had noted its shabby exterior, his observation can be contrasted with its new, neat appearance.

AW exulted in striding out upwards between the dry-built limestone walling of this delightful track and, 60 years on, it is easy to see why. Very quickly, any sense of bustle is left behind as you approach the quiet upland country and there is a growing sense of freedom. Or at least there should be – I suggest that if there isn't then your desires might be best served by returning to civilisation and finding the nearest amusement park. The steepness of the track lessens as it turns north-east and the way ahead can be seen following the gently undulating course between the parallel walls. Looking over the fine dry valley to the east, Pen-y-Ghent watches our every step. For the first mile of our trek to Foxup Moor we cannot expect to be alone as the track may well be populated with Pennine Way walkers and other trippers making their way up to Hull Pot – most, for some inexplicable reason, walking with their handbags.

After the Pennine Way branches off to the right at a gate, we only have the trippers to contend with, and most of those will be left behind as we press on beyond the great chasm that marks the end of Hull Pot Beck, where it sinks without trace into the limestone. AW's route is slightly unclear so I would suggest that we follow the path to the east of Hull Pot Beck until a stile is reached on the right. My only reason for this diversion is that we might enjoy a short, silent rest now that the crowds have gone, as the beck provides for a peaceful spot of foot-bathing in its cold clear waters. A clear path leads us eastwards to rejoin the bridleway that begins its long skirt around the north-western shoulder of Plover Hill. Turning left on the bridleway, our course is set by the wall that lies immediately to our right.

It ought to be pleasing to note that in the intervening 60 years some things have remained unchanged, but the extent of the morass that passes for a path is perhaps the exception that proves the rule. It was a squelching mire when AW passed this way and so it still is now, and I have to confess that in avoiding the worst of the bogs I fear that I added to them being slowly widened. It may be easier, as AW advocated, to accept soggy footwear but with many days and miles still to travel, the prospect of carrying a small part of Yorkshire in my boots does not appeal.

As we begin to round the north-west slopes of Plover Hill, the upper reaches of Littondale begin to come into view and Foxup Moor itself seems to stretch forever in all directions. We have been removed into a quiet world far from amusement parks both physically and spiritually. Bliss.

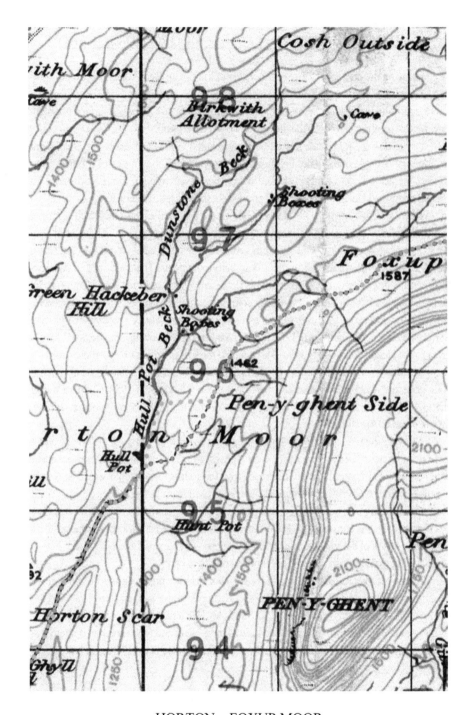

HORTON – FOXUP MOOR

DAY NO. 1/MAP NO. 4 FOXUP MOOR – HORSE HEAD

Following the contours to the southern side of the Foxup Beck valley, our route's previous quagmire has relented with the way underfoot becoming firmer and giving way to a more established track. The path maintains its altitude until 867761 when it turns northerly and we can see the steep climb that lies ahead up to Horse Head.

We can also see Littondale's last metropolis, Halton Gill, which sits on the break point on the northern side of the dale. Following the track through the lower fields brings us to Foxup, the last outpost of this unspoiled dale, where even walking the short distance on macadam toward Halton Gill is pleasant enough for there is little or no traffic.

When AW passed in 1938, Halton Gill served the local community with a chapel which doubled as a school. AW related the account of a curate who, in 1743, wrote of how he would serve both Halton Gill and Hubberholme and in so doing would traverse Horse Head Moor upon a white steed to minister to both settlements. The curate at that date was Reverend Miles Wilson; he served until his death in 1776. One of his sons went on to be tutor to William Pitt the Younger before becoming a canon at Windsor. Perhaps more striking was the successor to Reverend Miles – one Thomas Lindley who served the two communities for 70 years from 1777 to 1847 with records showing that he would walk over Horse Head Moor each Sunday. He provided the school services for all those years.

As with so many other changes that have had an impact upon the Dales, the chapel has long gone and is now a private house, ceasing its school function in 1958. Children would then have to head further down the dale to school; for many years the younger children would travel to Arncliffe, but that too closed in 2011.

Following the road toward Halton Gill, a gate is reached just short of the village and it is pleasing to note that the sign, which read 'Hawes' in AW's day, now rather more accurately proclaims 'Yockenthwaite via Horse Head Pass'. It is to Yockenthwaite that we are heading and our way up out of Littondale to the pass will seem longer than just 1 mile, for it follows a winding cart track that is unforgiving. I can only suggest several lingering rearward views for we are about to leave our second dale. We can also enjoy increasingly impressive views of the way we have come, culminating in the unmistakable form of Pen-y-ghent rearing its summit above the nearer horizon of Plover Hill.

A common feature of these upland areas is that field-boundary wallers are not known to flinch at the prospect of their trade being carried on in some inhospitable places and the summit of Horse Head is no exception. The track leads to a gate through a wall that extends as far as the eye can see, to the north-west over Horse Head and to the south east stretching out along the plateau-like moor top. The last ascent of the day is over so rest a little just as AW did at this very gate.

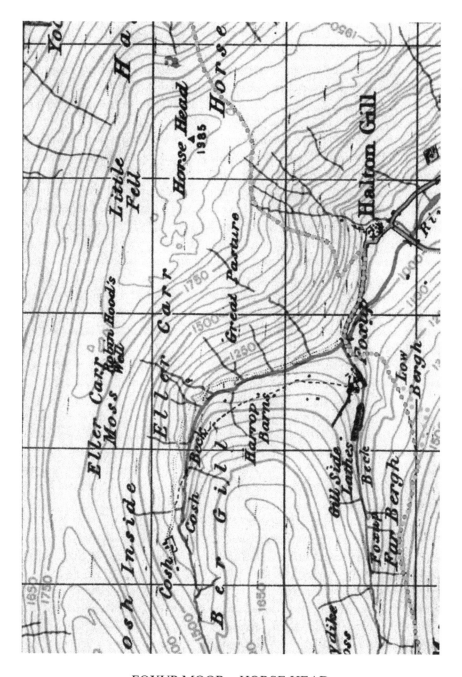

FOXUP MOOR – HORSE HEAD

DAY NO. 1/MAP NO. 5 HORSE HEAD – BUCKDEN

The descent from the gate on Horse Head is a joy not least for the fact that we can relax in the knowledge that the ascents are done for the day. The well-defined track ceases at the gate but a distinct bridleway leads clearly down and across Horse Head Moor to the farm buildings at Raisgill (incorrectly noted by AW as Ramsgill).

Upper Wharfedale lies below where we will encounter our third long distance path, the Dales Way. Walking two of its most beautiful miles will spare us the trials of the road walk from Raisgill to Buckden. 1938 might have seen little activity on this stretch of road but it is now a verge-less and well-used dales artery that is an anathema from a walker's point of view. It is foolhardy in the extreme to think that any pleasure can be gained at the end of a hard but enjoyable day by enduring the last few miles among motorists and groups of lycra-clad cyclists. No, at Raisgill turn left along the road the short distance to the tiny hamlet of Yockenthwaite where crossing the river and turning right takes us onto the Dales Way. After a little more than a mile we will approach what J B Priestley considered to be one of the prettiest places he ever came upon. For a man who had travelled extensively this was high praise indeed. So sincere were his sentiments that he requested that it be his final resting-place. Hubberholme and its "fine little old church" (J B Priestley, English Journey 1934) is a delight among delights. It seems likely that both JB and AW sat upon the bench just by the bridge and pondered and I suggest a similar momentary pause. It might not do any good but it certainly won't do any harm and it is a fine old bench in an idyllic spot.

For the first part of our final leg we must follow the road but in so doing we pass Grange Farm which, by a fairly uninteresting coincidence except for sad folk like me, is now the family home of the Falshaws. It was the paternal grandmother, Ada Falshaw, who had provided accommodation for AW all those years before at what was then "Prospect Farm". The farm was one of six at that time that operated in the village but it has gone the way of many other old dalesfolk houses; Prospect Farm, now known as Clifford House, is a nicely manicured self-catering cottage.

Ada didn't only provide accommodation for AW; she would often put up groups of cyclists for in the 1930's cycling had become a popular means of town dwellers experiencing the countryside. Indeed, earlier on this first day, it has been a group of noisy cyclists who has deterred AW from stopping at the café in Stainforth.

It is strange that there exists a further coincidence at Grange Farm which links back to J B Priestley. He stayed at the farm but sadly only after his death in 1984 – the church had not given the necessary approval prior to his ashes arriving in Wharfedale so he was forced to break his final journey while approval was sought.

Shortly beyond Grange Farm the path strikes off across the adjoining pastures to join the riverbank for the last half-mile of level walking to Buckden. At the road turn left into the village and the first day of our adventure is at an end.

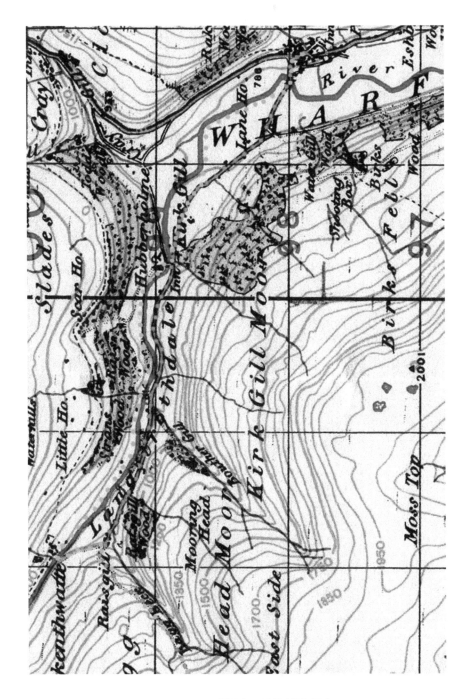

HORSE HEAD – BUCKDEN

DAY NO.2

BUCKDEN TO MUKER

DAY NO 2

BUCKDEN TO MUKER

The walking today is straightforward with easy route finding with tracks and roads to follow except for the last mile into Muker. The day is split into five legs as follows:

Leg	From:	To:
2 – 1	Buckden	Kidstones
2 – 2	Kidstones	Stalling Busk
2 – 3	Stalling Busk	Askrigg
2 – 4	Askrigg	Oxnop
2 – 5	Oxnop	Muker

The total distance is approximately 17 miles and takes us from Wharfedale, using the old Roman road from Buckden over Kidstones Fell, and via Semer Water in Raydale and on into Wensleydale. Crossing the River Ure, we then proceed up and over Askrigg Common and down the dramatic Oxnop Gill valley and into Muker in Swaledale.

Exploring a little in the village of Askrigg may delay us and as some of the hills are steep on this second day I suggest that eight hours is allowed for the day's walk.There is some unavoidable road walking so take care when among any traffic.

The map required for the day is from the 'Outdoor Leisure' series:

OL30   Yorkshire Dales (Northern & Central)

DAY NO. 2/MAP NO. 1 BUCKDEN – KIDSTONES

In 1938, Buckden was a very different place to the well-manicured village that now forms the last sizeable settlement in Wharfedale. By and large, it now caters for the tourist industry and is peppered with quaint guesthouses and second homes, and today there are now no working farms in the village.

Before starting out on his second day, AW called at the post office, which at that time was, coincidentally, run by Jimmy Falshaw of the same farming family that owned Prospect Farm. Mr Falshaw served in the forces during the ensuing war that pre-occupied AW's thoughts and his wife Cissie then ran the shop – she was remembered as being very patient with the Leeds Grammar School boys who were evacuated to Buckden House during the hostilities (as outlined in the memoirs of Hilda Christie).

Prior to the war, Buckden House had been the manorial home to Miss Elizabeth Stansfield until her death just prior to AW's visit. It then provided accommodation for evacuated children – the same children from Leeds Grammar School that Hilda Christie wrote about. After the Second World War, the building was privately owned until 1974 when it returned to accommodating children, this time as an outdoor education centre.

Formal education facilities ceased being provided in Buckden in 1933 when the school, near the car park at the northern end of the village, closed and it is from here that our route starts – at the north end of the car park, Buckden Rake strikes off northerly on the line of the Roman road that was part of the route from Ilkley (Olicana) to Bainbridge (Virosydum) and beyond.

When AW left Buckden, he retraced his steps to revisit Hubberholme and then proceeded across the head of the valley and up to Cray, requiring an unpleasantly busy walk up the main road out of Wharfedale. This divergence from his route avoids the busy road and allows us to enjoy treading the way of Romans many years before. The Buckden Rake track ascends steadily and as it turns north-east it follows the contours on a path high above Cray, across the valley.

By way of another coincidence the pub at Cray, the White Lion, is relevant on our journey – in Hilda Christie's account she refers to the boys being very keen on investigating the site of a 1942 plane crash. She is referring to the events of 30 January 1942, when a Polish-crewed Wellington bomber crashed on Buckden Pike in atrocious weather. All crew members were killed except the rear gunner, Joseph Fusniak, who, although badly injured followed the tracks of a fox. Remembering his Boy Scout days, he recalled that the fox would always try to find lower ground in such weather where food might be more plentiful. He was found by Nannie Parker, the daughter of the landlord, was rescued to the pub and survived his ordeal. Joseph returned on several occasions and in 1973 decided to build a memorial to those events and his lucky escape.

We must follow the road for a short distance before we arrive at a gate leading to Gilbert Lane signposted Bainbridge.

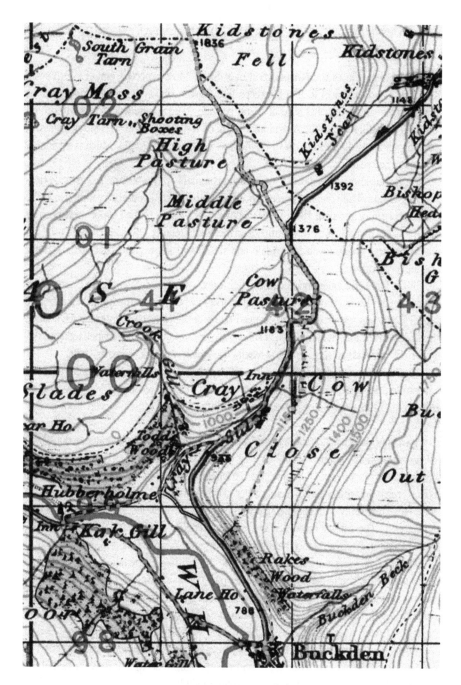

BUCKDEN – KIDSTONES

DAY NO. 2/MAP NO. 2 KIDSTONES – STALLING BUSK

The continuation of the Roman road over Stake Moss proceeds entirely unchanged from AW's description of it. It still sweeps like a green ribbon across the moor and the springy grass verges to either side of it still provide some respite from the stony central portion. There still remains the sensation of being on top of the world with the sky massive above us, all the while looking down on the new valley, Wensleydale, which is beginning to open out before us.

The track is known as Gilbert Lane, which presumably pays some regard to its destination, Bainbridge. The village provided poor law accommodation at the workhouse in the nineteenth century and until 1869 it was what was known as a Gilbert Union workhouse – it seems likely that this may have influenced the track's name. The walled green road begins to descend gently towards Raydale and we should follow it toward Stalling Busk, ignoring any junctions.

Gilbert Lane continues and becomes High Lane where, at a gate, it joins Stake Road. There is a path leading down through Stalling Busk where refreshment can be had in the village; I only suggest pressing on because I had a desire to reach Bainbridge for a lunch stop. If you divert into Stalling Busk, a short walk leads to the original chapel, today standing in ruins having been replaced by St Matthews, which was built as late as 1909.

From the ruined chapel, there is a low-level path that leads along the eastern shore of Semerwater; our route remains on the more elevated metalled road as cars are few and far between, and the surrounding panoramas are all the more spectacular seen from greater height.

From our raised position there is a fine view over the lake of Semerwater, about which AW was, unusually, wrong; he had stated it is the one sheet of water that the Dales could show. In fact, it is the second largest lake – Malham Tarn being the larger. Much folklore abounds regarding the origin of Semerwater. There have been stories of a sunken village and a magical traveller who conjured a great flood after the local folk had shown him a lack of generosity. The story is recounted in the poem 'The Lost Village of Semer' written by Glynne Hughes, a copy of which hangs in the Rose and Crown at Bainbridge.

Glaciation provides the scientist's answer to the forming of the lake with the Raydale glacier trapped by the larger Wensleydale ice pack. Moraine was dropped into the valley forming a natural lake which eventually broke out of its containment just south of Bainbridge with the resultant narrow, steep-sided valley through which the River Bain, England's shortest river, flows into the Ure.

However, excavations carried out just one year before AW's trip following a period of very low water levels found evidence of an Iron Age village on what is now the bed of the lake. So perhaps the story of the mystical traveller might be true!

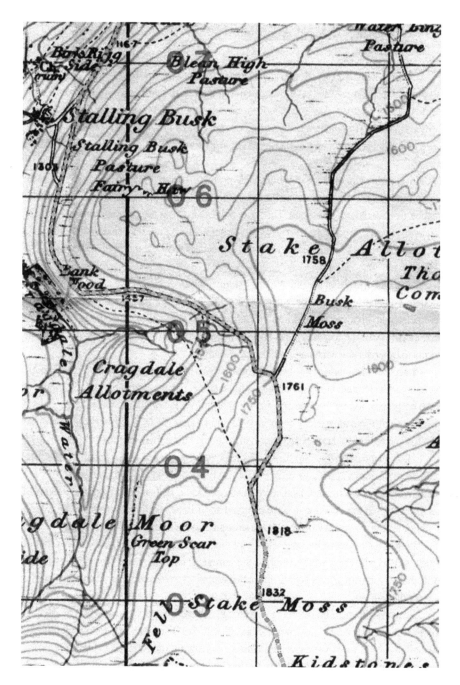

KIDSTONES – STALLING BUSK

DAY NO. 2/MAP NO. 3 STALLING BUSK – ASKRIGG

Leaving Stalling Busk, the road generally descends to the River Bain outlet at the northern end of Semerwater. AW had been told by a local that Semerwater rivalled Windermere in its beauty – AW's curt judgement was that Semerwater was a 'flooded field'. Perhaps his view might change if he could compare them now for I am sure he would believe that Windermere's appeal had lessened in inverse proportion to the vast increase in tourism.

A riverside path leads off down Raydale northerly toward Bainbridge, 2.5 miles away – this makes the Bain England's shortest main river and the walk beside it is a tranquil saunter that should not be rushed. The route pulls away from the river and the path climbs to circumvent an impossibly narrow ravine through which the infant river has been forced to pass. After a short distance we return to a metalled road for the final walk down into Bainbridge.

As we pass the site of the old White Lion Inn, long since closed, we come across a very modern addition to Bainbridge – the Archimedes screw that uses river water to provide hydroelectricity that can be sold into the national grid. It provides sufficient power to provide electricity to the local residents and, as we shall see across the valley at Askrigg, this seems to be a return to what had been the case many years prior.

Our route to Bainbridge has been along what was a part of the Roman road from Ilkley and the fort on Brough Hill (Bainbridges's full name is Brough-by-Bainbridge) is known to have been occupied by the Romans. On the map of AW's era it was simply referred to as 'Roman Camp' but after excavations in 1925 and into the 1930s it is thought to be the site of a Roman settlement known as Virosidvm, as noted on the modern map.

In the village itself, the map shows a location referred as 'P A Instn' and this provides a little more of Bainbridge's interesting history. AW mentioned a workhouse and today the building now known as High Hall served as the workhouse. Its function gradually changed until 1930 when the Poor Laws were changed and former workhouses became known as 'Public Assistance Institutions', hence the reference on the map.

The Rose and Crown beckons and I trust that we have plenty of time to order a spot of lunch with a quiet drink while admiring the famous Bainbridge horn, which hangs on the wall that was blown each evening from September as guidance to any travellers on the surrounding moors.

The next settlement on our route is Askrigg, and we are lucky because we can pick up the line of the old railway just over the bridge over the River Ure. We follow the line for about half a mile when we arrive at a cluster of unsightly industrial units, which stand on the site of the old station, and at the eastern end of them we turn left and join the road leading into the village.

STALLING BUSK – ASKRIGG

DAY NO. 2/MAP NO. 4 ASKRIGG – OXNOP

The last passenger travelled into Askrigg via the railway in 1954, and although freight continued from quarrying works, the final death knell came in 1964 with the line at Askrigg being lifted. There has been a move to reopen the line as a heritage railway and this has been done as far as Redmire but further progress west toward Garside requires considerable reconstruction of bridges and viaducts.

We arrive in the village crossing the Mill Gill Bridge, where just a few hundred yards upstream there was once something akin to a forerunner of the Bainbridge hydro scheme. West Mill, as marked on the map, had become a saw mill and the owner, Mr W. H. Burton, had used a race on the gill to provide electricity to run the mill. By 1910 he had extended the output to provide electricity to the village. Burton died just a year before AW's visit but his sons had succeeded him, and this private power source continued until 1949 when the national grid reached Askrigg.

Askrigg itself is a delightful settlement with a sense of being a living and breathing community rather than displaying the museum-like qualities of Buckden. The village was once the market town serving Upper Wensleydale prior to Hawes taking on the mantle on the arrival of the first turnpike in the eighteenth century. The village was, in long past days, at the centre of skilled trades, particularly clock making, with successive generations producing high-quality long-case clocks that are famous the world over. The trade began to dwindle toward the end of the eighteenth century and perhaps there is a connection with the arrival of the turnpike with Askrigg's commercial importance being diminished, but this may be only conjecture.

The increase in visitor numbers has resulted in a proliferation of shops, tearooms, inns and a general feeling of bustle. The tourists who travel here to visit Darrowby and the buildings used in the television series All Creatures Great and Small have, in more recent times, supplemented this sense of activity. Skeldale House is now a boarding house standing in a commanding position opposite the twelfth-century church and has provided the impetus for the tripper bric-a-brac shops.

If you are tempted to buy a trinket, don't buy anything too heavy for the next mile or so our stamina will be sorely tested as we make our way up and onto Askrigg Common. Our way out of the village follows a quiet minor road signposted Muker and it immediately takes a steep and twisting course. You might want to rest and look back and consider what it might have been about Wensleydale that disappointed AW. In his account he concluded that it held little to entice the visitor and that he had looked back on this climb more times than the view merited.

While our route aims to avoid road-walking, there is no path that links Wensleydale and Swaledale, but as the road is so quiet it is a suitable route. After a long traverse of open moorland the burgeoning view ahead is of Swaledale. At a fork in the road the left branch heads downhill with Oxnop Gill to the right and Muker our next stop.

ASKRIGG – OXNOP

DAY NO. 2/MAP NO. 5 OXNOP – MUKER

The road, known as the Gorge Road, continues down the western side of Oxnop Gill with views opening up eastwards down Swaledale. Sight of our destination remains hidden for the moment behind the shoulder of Oxnop Side. AW had followed the Gorge Road to its junction with the valley road and then followed what is now the B6270 into Muker. To take that route is unpleasantly busy with few places of refuge and I suggest a more amenable route to Muker be taken. In assuming that you have your 1:25000 OS map, I also assume you will be able to find your way via the field paths (starting at 925973) to arrive at the track leading to The Rigg near the bridge crossing Straw Beck and into Muker village.

Eons ago, instead of crossing a tributary beck we would have been crossing the River Swale, but glacial action rerouted the river around the eastern flank of Kisdon, a route that we will follow on our third day.

When AW stayed in this delightful Swaledale village he did so at the house of the Harkers and they spent a tense evening anxious about developments in Europe. David Harker was his host and his house, South View, is the property adjacent to the church that AW referred to. The family name Harker is longstanding in the dale and David Harker was a stalwart of the community, playing euphonium in the famous Muker Silver Band (referred to in G. Bernard Wood's Yorkshire Villages as the 'Old Roy').

Wood's book, published in 1971, referred to the occasion a few years earlier when he had spent a day with the Harkers. Wood's specific interest centred around another renowned local – Mr Cherry Kearton, who had been born in Thwaite and schooled in Muker. Mr Kearton, and his elder brother, Richard, were forerunners of modern naturalists and their skills were honed in the delightful environment of Upper Swaledale. There still exist memorials to the brothers on the building that served as the school. Such is his renown that the Royal Geographic Society still gives the Cherry Kearton Medal for achievements in photographing natural history.

In addition to providing boarding for AW, Cherry Kearton also lodged at South View as a guest of David Harker while supervising shoots for an autobiographical film in later life. David Harker had even sought out a local lad, Lancelot Guy, who would play the part of a younger Cherry.

Muker remains very much as it was in those days when the Crisis was the talk of South View during the evening of 26 September 1938 when AW calculated he had but four days to live.

Hopefully nothing so dramatic will occur during our stay. Celebrate the end of Day 2 but not too much for tomorrow is a harder day – 23 miles that will take us from Swaledale, over Tan Hill and on into Teesdale by way of Bowes.

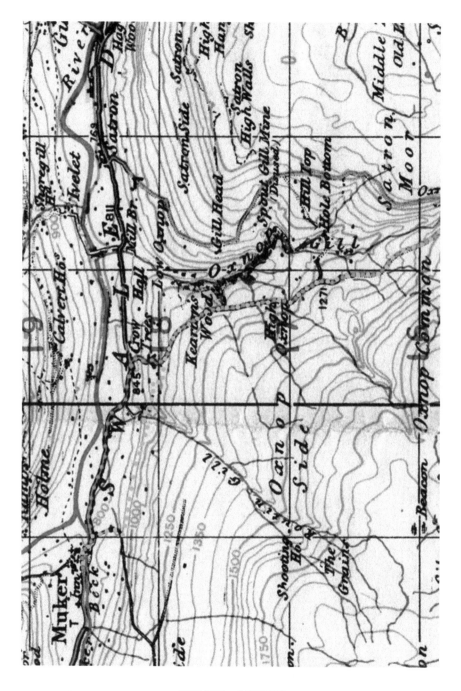

OXNOP – MUKER

DAY NO. 3

MUKER TO ROMALDKIRK

DAY NO. 3

MUKER TO ROMALDKIRK

The walking is getting longer and the route-finding slightly more troublesome, especially as we cross Cotherstone Moor. We share our way with the famous but very boggy Pennine Way for a few miles and finish the day following the lesser-known but very picturesque Teesdale Way. (We even spend a few yards along probably the greatest long-distance path that is associated with AW; the Coast to Coast path is joined just north of the River Swale at Kisdon Force.) I have walked neither but from the muddy evidence both on and in my boots the Teesdale Way holds the greater appeal. The day is spilt into seven legs as follows:

Leg	From:	To:
3 – 1	Muker	Keld
3 – 2	Keld	Tan Hill
3 – 3	Tan Hill	Sleightholme
3 – 4	Sleightholme	Gilmonby Moor
3 – 5	Gilmonby Moor	High Crag
3 – 6	High Crag	Cotherstone
3 – 7	Cotherstone	Romaldkirk

The total distance is approximately 23 miles and takes us out of Swaledale, the last of the steep-sided valleys, and via the Pennine Way into a moorland landscape that is attractive only in its barrenness. It could not be said to be pretty, and it certainly isn't beautiful, but it presents a fine challenge for this our longest day so far. Our route leads us over Stonesdale Moor, onto Sleightholme Moor, around Gilmonby Moor and finally over Cotherstone Moor before descending into the valley of the River Tees (much improved from the time AW berated it). There is little to cause serious delay en route although it would be remiss not to call in at the Tan Hill Inn for a quick drink, it being England's highest inn and all that (well, it certainly provides a good enough excuse as far as I'm concerned). Apart from the small village store in Bowes there is also little opportunity to acquire provisions of any sort so either take a packed lunch or eat either early at the Tan Hill Inn or late at the Unicorn Inn at Bowes.

Two maps are required for the day from the 'Outdoor Leisure' series:

     OL30   Yorkshire Dales (Northern & Central).

     OL31   North Pennines (Teesdale and Weardale)

Allowing for some slowing due to route finding, I would suggest the day's walk will take us ten hours.

DAY NO. 3/MAP NO. 1 MUKER – KELD

As with Halton Gill and Buckden, Muker is another Dales village that has lost its school; today local children having to travel down the dale for primary education and as far as Richmond for secondary level. The likes of the Kearton brothers will no doubt go the way of many other modern village dwellers and move away as their wings are stretched for them during education.

Before leaving Muker, there is a further association with the past and more particularly with Mr and Mrs Harker. I found it rather cathartic to visit their joint gravestone in St Mary's cemetery, which shows that Mr Harker reached his eightieth year before his death in 1968. Seeing their names carved as two of the people who came close to AW during his journey helps to place a perspective that connects then and now. If you are to visit then please do so with care and respect.

It is pleasing that after having walked for too many miles on the previous day on hard surfaces, AW left made-up roads behind and struck out northwards from Muker on what he described as a very fine walk alongside the river. The path is well trodden (and for the first fields proceeds along a stone-flagged course) presenting no navigation difficulties – opposite the Swinner Gill valley our way leaves the flat river plain and follows the path uphill to join a more definite path that descends from our left, this being the point at which we have rejoined the Pennine Way and will remain on it as far as Sleightholme.

It is along this stretch that the Kearton brothers practiced their art of naturalist photography. It was an art that they took sufficiently seriously to have been known to set up a hide in what might best be described as a pantomime cow! Back in the day this would have been quite a feat to include a large glass-plate camera, which undoubtedly would have required a tripod. There is an archive photograph of the brothers extending a tripod with birch branches, with one brother precariously standing on the other's shoulders to get the image of a bird nesting.

We follow the Pennine Way down to the River Swale and over the footbridge, immediately beyond which we are walking on yet another path with an even greater association with AW – the Coast to Coast Path, which was probably his crowning glory. It shares our route for the short distance to East Stonesdale Farm.

Where we made our way down to the footbridge we parted company with AW, for he continued on through Keld and once again accepted the relative displeasure of following a hard road surface. In fact, the great majority of the remainder of his third day's walk was spent either on, or at the side of, roads or hard tracks.

A short detour into the village of Keld will show why AW thought that time here was measured in centuries. It is the last grouped habitation within the dale and has seen the passing of all shops, the inns marked on the old maps are no more and even the youth hostel closed in 2006.

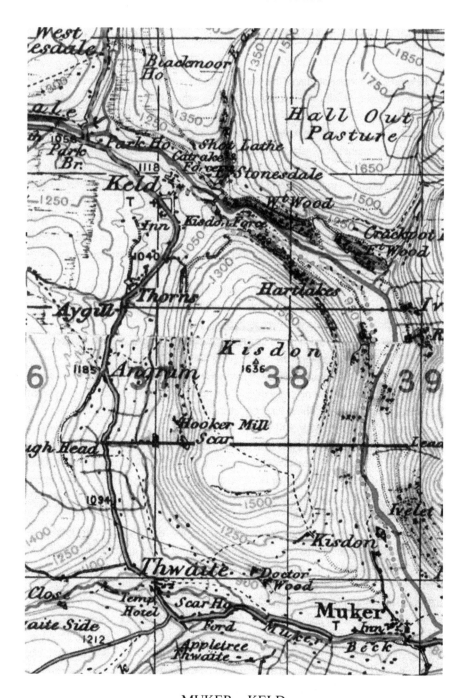

MUKER – KELD

DAY NO. 3/MAP NO. 2 KELD – TAN HILL

Beyond East Stonesdale Farm the gradient lessens and the walled meadows become fewer, being replaced with the increasingly wild moorland that will accompany us until within sight of Bowes. Mould Gill marks the definite point at which we enter the open moorland. Should it be that we pass up this eastern side of West Stones Dale after a period of rain then we might have wished to trudge up the road as AW had done, for the ground underfoot is reduced to great patches of bog and mire. There is respite from the mire as we reach an old packhorse trail which will lead us all the way to Tan Hill, the junction of four such trails from days long ago.

Perhaps we should look on the bright side, though; as we have joined the Pennine Way there is little chance of becoming lost for all we have to do is follow the cagoule in front. It is the interminable 'Good mornings' that start to wear a little thin after meeting the umpteenth group of walkers coming the other way.

The terrain might be boot-clingingly unpalatable and the way ahead might seem to hold a promise of similar but take heart, the Tan Hill Inn is only an hour away and, as we climb, the rearward views become more rewarding.

Evidence of mining and quarrying activity is plentiful hereabouts and in these surroundings it is easy to imagine the harshness of the life that the workers would have endured. The workings left behind did not receive mention in AW's account, but that was probably because, on his journey, visibility was so poor he would not have seen them from across the valley. Tan Hill Colliery had been abandoned in 1935 but the adjacent King's Pit was in use with one sole worker until 1945.

The coal was of poor quality, known as crow coal. This became a major issue during the Industrial Revolution as steam engines required a better, cleaner burning coal. The Durham coal mines fared better with their better quality coal being used for the new engines on the Stockton and Darlington railway and probably spelled the beginning of the end for commercial production at Tan Hill.

The adversity of the environment is aptly described by Mr Jack Rukin, the local postman who told of the sheer effort needed to fulfill his postal duties in 1936. His round took him on foot from Keld up to Tan Hill Inn, where he was a welcome visitor and a link to the outside world. The inn had no wireless and, after the mines closed, this isolation required a hardy soul to withstand the day-to-day rigours.

In over thirty years of deliveries, Mr Rukin was presented with some seriously unpleasant weather, using a pony if the weather was sufficiently inclement. It is a tribute to him that he reported only being prevented on one occasion from reaching his destination. He, along with other Keld folk, featured in a 1935 radio broadcast about life in the dale and his father was included in the broadcast as having worked for sixty years at the Tan Hill Colliery. Mr Rukin senior was eighty-eight in 1936 and presumably left the colliery when it was abandoned in 1935 (at the age of eighty-seven!).

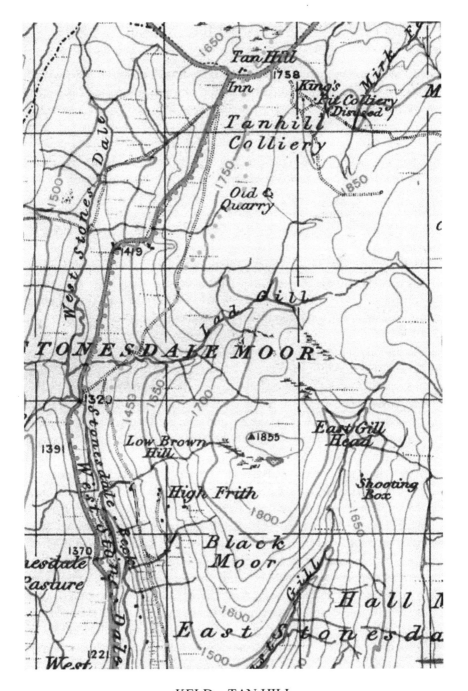

KELD – TAN HILL

DAY NO. 3/MAP NO. 3 TAN HILL – SLEIGHTHOLME

At Tan Hill there were once a number of cottages housing miners but these were demolished once the mines were abandoned, leaving only the inn standing in its splendid isolation with the claim as being the highest public house in England. As reported by Jack Rukin, it clearly took a strong character to cater with both the 'locals' and the inn's situation.

Once such innkeeper was Mrs Susan Peacock, who was the landlady just prior to AW's visit and had been since 1903 when she had moved here from the Cat Holes Inn near Keld. AW wrote of his encounter but referred to the innkeeper as 'a grizzled companiable fellow', and in this he would have been referring to Mr Michael Peacock, whom Mrs Peacock had married after the death of her first husband, leaving her to bring up their three daughters.

Mr Peacock had been, in the early part of the twentieth century, the owner of the nearby King's Pit colliery and he joined Susan at the inn until her death in May 1937. Such was her standing that the funeral was a large affair, the cortege starting out from Tan Hill before proceeding down to the Congregational Church in Keld for the burial.

Susan Peacock's hardiness appears also to have been passed down to her daughters, for Jack Rukin recalled that they would walk each day down to school in Keld (another school that has long since closed).

In the days of waning mining activity, the Peacocks were able to establish a viable business, probably owing some success to the increase in motoring and also more folks getting out and about hiking. Mrs Peacock was also adroit at marketing the inn by featuring in radio broadcasts telling the listener of the quiet life and arousing a curiosity that brought visitors to the inn to witness it for themselves.

Susan Peacock must indeed have been a strong character. It has been long-reported that she kept a loaded revolver behind the bar and was not afraid to threaten to use it to make sure that her message was understood were a customer to become unruly through drink.

While at the inn, AW had discussed the fact that the county boundary between Yorkshire and Durham followed the course of the River Tees. This remained so until 1974 with the county boundary changes; on leaving the inn (and, incidentally, the Yorkshire Dales National Park) we are now within the boundaries of County Durham. The Pennine Way, which we are continuing to follow, bears left onto the old packhorse route towards Bowes.

In AW's Pennine Way Companion he likens the next stretch as being like walking in either porridge or oxtail soup, depending upon the weather. It might be wise to heed his words and take the alternative (and the route taken by AW in any case) in following the road. As he wrote in the companion, 'no-one need ever know.'

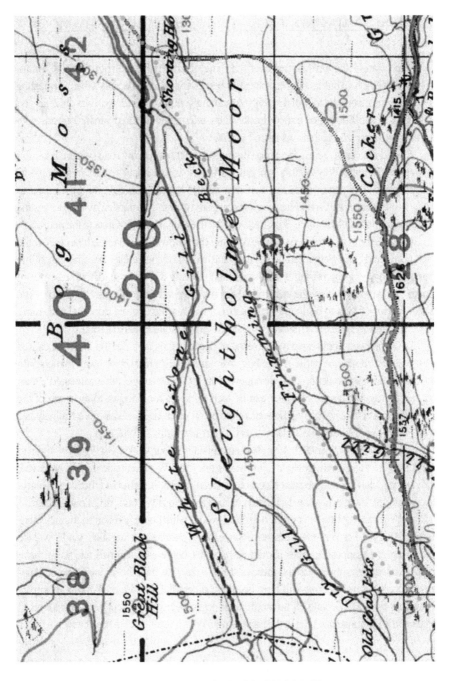

TAN HILL – SLEIGHTHOLME

DAY NO. 3/MAP NO. 4 SLEIGHTHOLME – GILMONBY MOOR

I am aware that I have skirted over the route description of the path from the inn towards Sleightholme but its unpleasantness is best overlooked, especially when contrasting it with the interesting history of Tan Hill. Assuming you have found your way thus far you will have, at 935091, joined a moor track which, after a few hundred yards, connects with the alternative road route that was taken by AW.

Beyond the convergence, our route lies as a distinct but narrow road (we are back following the Pennine Way) with a random patchwork of macadam repairs in amongst its stony surface. The patchwork gives way to a fully metalled surface as we draw nearer to Sleightholme Farm and soon after we part company with the Pennine Way as it leaves the road and follows Sleightholme Beck to its confluence with the River Greta to the north.

It is something of a mystery why AW chose the follow the road rather than follow the path northwards; it was marked on his map and would of course later become part of the Pennine Way. More surprising is the fact that in following the minor road north east toward Bowes, he would walk off the eastern edge of his map and have to walk 'blind' for some distance (Bowes was to be found on OS sheet No. 14 which he did not have with him). Indeed, he would walk the remainder of his third day without access to a map.

As we proceed north-easterly, the sense of peace begins to suffer the intrusion caused by the distant rumble of traffic on the busy A66, now only a mile or so away to the north; the road is now a thundering dual carriageway. In 1938 AW might have witnessed a train on the railway, the course of which can be seen in places running just to the north of the River Greta, but like so many others encountered on our route the Stainmore Railway has long since closed. The Bowes to Barras section last saw traffic in 1962.

It is perhaps coincidental that, while on many days of our walk we will bear witness to the demise of a great railway legacy, just weeks prior to AW's excursion the UK achieved, through the Mallard, an unbeaten locomotive speed record. It seems sad that only twenty-five years later there began the decimation of such a previously proud part of our heritage.

In AW's account he refers to a delightful wood, which clearly refers to the glade enclosing Huggill Force – the trees have since been cleared and no such wood will be encountered. Disappearing trees should perhaps not come as a surprise for, as we have made our way over the moorland these past few miles, we have been doing so via Stainmore Forest, yet not one tree will have been encountered! There are many other examples of treeless forests, especially in the north, their origin being the subject of discussion as to whether the clearance has been at the hand of man or as a result of climatic change.

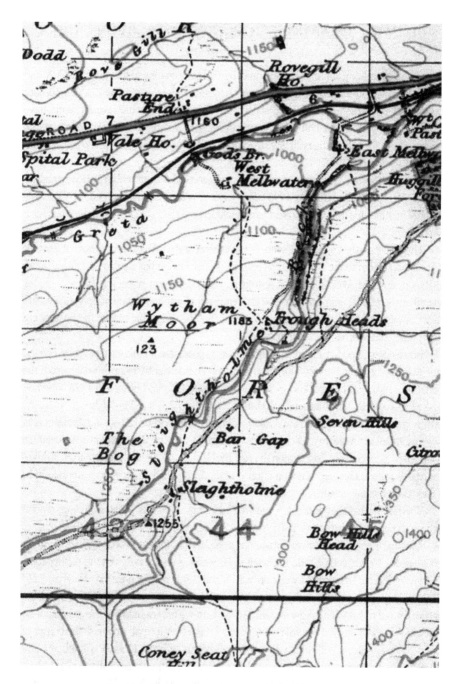

SLEIGHTHOLME – GILMONBY MOOR

DAY NO. 3/MAP NO. 5 GILMONBY MOOR – HIGH CRAG

Our easy walking continues on the quiet byroad still seeming to turn away, as AW had noted, from taking a direct route to Bowes. As Gilmonby is approached, AW's account referred to 'picturesque cottages and stately residences', one of which would surely have been Gilmonby Hall. The hall is no more, having been demolished in 1945, but over the bridge and up the hill on the north side the village of Bowes is probably little changed from when he was here in 1938.

At the crossroads, a left turn leads up the main street and forms a quiet backwater as the village was finally bypassed in 1993 after years of protest from local people (Hansards records in 1982 that one such protest even included the road actually being blocked for a short period).

There is, though, a sense of a village whose heart and soul has been removed. Perhaps the improvements to the A66 have resulted in a safer village but also one that has had its lifeblood removed. What remains is a street that is incongruous in that it is far too wide for the village's relative unimportance and the remnants of a filling station simply adds to the air of desolation. My last visit was in 1998 so I can only hope that maybe the intervening years have seen a turnaround in fortunes.

Bowes' past is perhaps more interesting than its present, with this interest centred on the public house bearing the very individual name of The Ancient Unicorn. It dates from the sixteenth century and is best known for playing host to Charles Dickens in 1838, when he visited to research the infamous 'Yorkshire Schools' for his novel Nicholas Nickleby, which is said to be based upon the dubious educational system meted out at establishments such as at Bowes Academy. Dickens was appalled at what he found and it is believed his 'Wackford Squeers' was based upon the real-life William Shaw, and the character 'Smike' derived from one George Ashton, a pupil who died while at the school and is buried in St Giles' church in the village.

The pub is also a subject to a variety of hauntings within its walls, including, among others, a young lad who patrols the cellar.

Leaving the main street, we retrace our steps back to the crossroads and leave AW's route again,, for we certainly do not want to be walking on the busy road to Cotherstone. Following the old main road for a short way, a path leads off north-easterly to Myre Keld Farm, requiring a careful crossing of the A66. Turning onto the farm track and crossing the line of the old railway we follow it to the A67, where we turn right to pick up a footpath on the left. A path leads over two stiles to a sleeper bridge over a small stream in the corner of the next field. After a half-mile, where the wall begins to bend, look for a field gate and after passing through it take the path heading straight down the stream valley toward Nabb Bridge. The path then proceeds directly to the buildings in front, High Crag. Passing through the gate to the right of the buildings, the cart track heads north northeast downhill towards Low Crag.

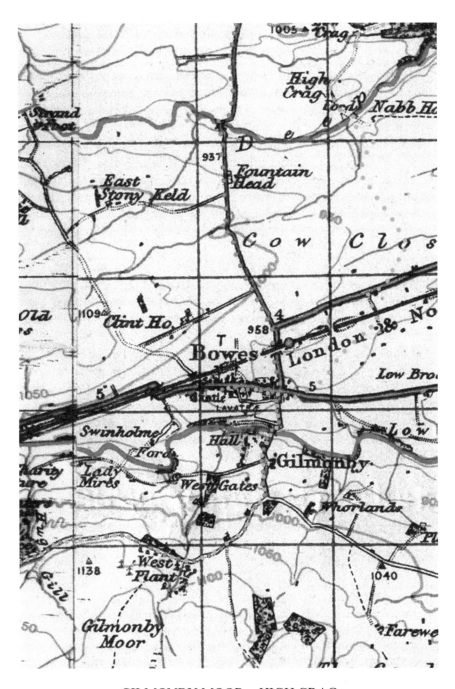

GILMONBY MOOR – HIGH CRAG

DAY NO. 3/MAP NO. 6 HIGH CRAG – COTHERSTONE

In avoiding the road walk from Bowes to Cotherstone, it has been necessary to depart from the description of historical associations of the route to more usual geographical guidance, and it is unfortunate that this section continues the need to guide rather than entertain (hopefully).

Somewhat confusingly, there are two Low Crags marked on the map – the one we are seeking is at 002162, after which the path leads as a bridleway around the southern face of the large barn and follows a clear track on the south side of Crag Pond through a enchantingly peaceful wood of silver birches. At a fork in the paths keep to the bridleway, turning north, and maintain a northerly course aiming for the western extent of a small wood that lies ahead. The track become metalled and descends to cross Gill Beck before ascending again to join Lartington Green Lane.

Turning right on the road, after 200 yards a path to the left continues our northern course and follows a wall while descending steeply into the wooded valley of Scur Beck. Crossing the beck, the path continues up the slope to Naby, after which the farm track heads north with the unsightly industrial works to the east. The ugly silo-type structures do at least act as a useful landmark.

Opposite the northern edge of the works' fencing, the track divides and our route is to turn east until we come to the next (broken-down) field boundary where we turn north, arriving at a stile after approximately 400 yards. The path then descends towards a small footbridge across Lance Beck. After crossing the bridge, keep to the right of the building ahead, following its boundary wall to a stile in the left corner of the field. A well-trodden path then leads to a stile to the embankment of the disused Tees Valley branch line. We can choose to either follow to line or cross the embankment; whichever way is chosen we will rejoin the road taken by AW as we approach Cotherstone. We will revisit this old railway track bed again on day four.

Cotherstone did not find favour with AW. He considered it to be too well-to-do for his liking, where the residents would be silently peering at him from behind chintz curtains and if any were to offer accommodation there would be disquiet among the other residents. In 1938 AW would still have been walking within the North Riding of Yorkshire and would do so as far as Middleton in Teesdale. For our walk, the boundary changes of 1974 mean that we have been in County Durham from Tan Hill onwards

Cotherstone is renowned for its cheese, made here for hundreds of years. Rather similar to Wensleydale, it was only actively marketed to differentiate from its better-known rival in the early 1900s, with one major local producer being the Birketts at West Park. Production ceased just after AW's visit with the onset of the war and only started again is earnest in the later years of the twentieth century.

HIGH CRAG – COTHERSTONE

DAY NO. 3/MAP NO.7 COTHERSTONE – ROMALDKIRK

Cotherstone is a delightful Teesdale village and, unlike other villages we have visited, it has the rare accolade that, rather than having closed its school, it actually opened a new primary school in 1965.

Cotherstone is also the home to the famous spinster Hannah Hauxwell, who moved here in 1998 after having to yield to old age; her previously lonely life up on the moors at Low Birk Hatt Farm had become harder as each winter took its toll. She remains one of those Dales folk who will be forever remembered fondly for her television appearances portraying a lifestyle that would leave the rest of us tired just watching.

When we approached Cotherstone we did so using the old railway track bed and it is possible to simply continue on what is now the Tees Railway Path through to day's end. However, as we follow the railway path on Day 4 I suggest we make for the riverside path and, in so doing, we share AW's route for half a mile through the village. We must leave him again unless you have a desire to inhale exhaust fumes for he trudged his way along the B road to Romaldkirk (he was still walking off the eastern edge of his most easterly map). A little way beyond the post office, opposite the Fox and Hounds, a lane to the right leads down toward the castle standing atop its seemingly impregnable natural buttress. It was obviously not wholly impregnable, for it now lies in ruins.

Our walk continues along the Teesdale Way on the western bank of the River Tees and we soon arrive at another of the so called 'Yorkshire Schools'. Woden Croft Academy now provides rather more pleasant self-catering accommodation than might have been afforded to its inmates back in the days when it was established by one Edward Simpson. He was master until his death in 1821, after which his son took over the reins and would have been in charge when Charles Dickens visited in the line of research for Nicholas Nickleby. Such schools were generally portrayed as Dotheboys Hall within the Dickens novel and the ensuing outcry essentially spelt the end of the academy regime.

A little way beyond Woden Croft, keeping to the river path, a short diversion to the river bank reveals the rock formation known as 'The Fairy Cupboards', a local Victorian tourist attraction formed from eroded bedrock. Around the riverbends the path then leaves the bank and ascends to Low Garth, a fine long house that is now derelict, and we are nearing the end of Day 3.

Continuing uphill from Low Garth, the path crosses two fields and arrives at Sennings Lane, a rough woodland lane which leads directly to the village of Romaldkirk, emerging very close to the Kirk Inn. It was at this inn that AW stayed after he had arrived in darkness and spent the silent evening listening to the tick of the clock with no other patrons visiting the inn.

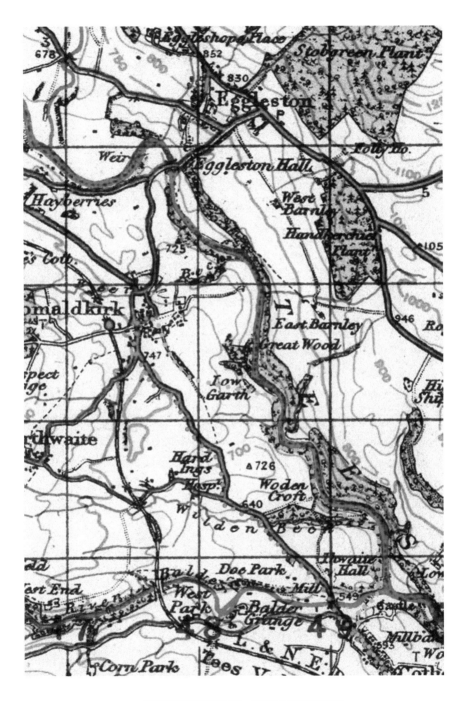

COTHERSTONE – ROMALDKIRK

DAY NO. 4

ROMALDKIRK TO
BLANCHLAND

DAY NO. 4

ROMALDKIRK TO BLANCHLAND

O n Day 4 AW walked more miles than on any other day. Frankly, he walked a few too many and I suggest that a reasonable goal for the day would be to reach Rookhope. Day 5, as walked by AW, only amounted to 10 miles, so increasing it by a further five leads to a more equitable split of daily distances. However, for accuracy's sake, I have described Day 4 as undertaken by AW. In addition, Rookhope has rather more choice of accommodation than offered by Blanchland.

In following the AW destination, the day is spilt into eight legs as follows:

Leg	From:	To:
4 – 1	Romaldkirk	Mickleton
4 – 2	Mickleton	Middleton-in-Teesdale
4 – 3	Middleton-in-Teesdale	Broadley's Gate
4 – 4	Broadley's gate	Swinhope Head
4 – 5	Swinhope Head	Westgate
4 – 6	Westgate	Rookhope
4 – 7	Rookhope	Bolt's Law
4 – 8	Bolt's Law	Blanchland

The full distance is approximately 26 miles, with the route starting easily enough, revisiting the Pennine Way along one of its prettier sections before undertaking the climb out of Teesdale and over Swinhope Moor and down into Weardale. The initially uninspiring Weardale develops into a delightful valley walk before we make our way up and over Scarsike Head to Rookhope. From Rookhope, the going becomes decidedly unfriendly as our way picks a tortured route through ancient lead-mining country to traverse 5 miles of wild moorland to Blanchland. This is another reason to consider pausing overnight at Rookhope and tackling this more difficult section afresh the following morning.

There is plenty of opportunity to purchase provisions in Middleton-in-Teesdale, albeit slightly off our route. Apart from that, our brushes with civilisation are few. There is no welcoming inn en route except for one that lies somewhat off our path in Westgate, so a packed lunch is called for.

Two maps are required for the day. The first is from the 'Outdoor Leisure' series:

OL31   North Pennines

There is also a small section north of Westgate that requires a map from the "Explorer" series:

307   Consett and Derwent Reservoir

Some of the walking is unfortunately along roads but they are very quiet with the road over Swinhope Head being gated and little used by cars. Depending on your choice of overnight break, the distances are as follows:

Romaldkirk–Rookhope	21 miles – allow 9 hours
Romaldkirk–Blanchland	26 miles – allow 12 hours

Horton Scar Lane

DAY NO. 4/MAP NO.1 ROMALDKIRK – MICKLETON

Romaldkirk is a quiet village with two greens, both of which retain an air of tranquility as the road to Middleton and beyond runs on a course that bypasses them. The water pump and village stocks give greater authenticity to the sensation that time has stood still. The only evidence of modern life is the four-wheel drive vehicles visiting the Rose and Crown after a day's shooting and the rather incongruous street lamp standards.

Like many other rural settlements, Romaldkirk has ceased to be a centre for employment for there is little work for the local folk as there once was. In 1823, the village would have been largely self-supporting with a doctor, five farmers, three masons, two shoemakers, three shopkeepers and one butcher, two weavers, a blacksmith and three wheelwrights. These tradespeople are long gone and the village has largely become the domain of the retired.

While staying at the Kirk Inn, AW wrote of the impoverished landlady and how the place had an eerie, hushed silence, all except for the ticking of the large inn clock. He was correct in his assertion that she was a widow and he was correct in that she had two daughters. He had wondered 'what blight lay over the house' and never did discover the secret as to why the inn was so avoided by the locals.

Joyce Hughes (née Bainbridge) was brought up in the village and in 1998 she kindly shed a little light that would help solve the mystery. She was of the same age as the Kirk Inn girls, Beryl and Jean, and recalled that they were among the first owners of bicycles in the village. She also recalled that the landlady, Mrs Walker, who had moved from Derbyshire, was a widower, her husband having been a retired policeman who died at about the same time as AW's visit. She believed that they had only recently taken over the management so perhaps this would readily explain both the lack of locals (newcomers not having been accepted) and the sombre air. Joyce was not kindly in her assessment of AW's judgement.

AW had once again decided to walk along macadam, firstly via Mickleton then through Middleton and beyond to Newbiggin before then ascending to Swinhope. It is likely that in Romaldkirk he still had no map for the village is just off the map's eastern edge until part-way to Mickleton. We are fortunate for we can savour what rail travellers once enjoyed by following the Tees Railway Path to its terminus. Access to the track is via the minor road heading west, where signage will direct around the former station buildings, now a private house, and onto the track as it bends away up the dale.

A little way along the track and there is a connection to even earlier times, when Romaldkirk lost one-third of its population to the plague. One survivor was Grace Scott, who built a mud hut and only returned to the village when the disease has passed. The farm built on the same site became known as 'Grace's Cottage'.

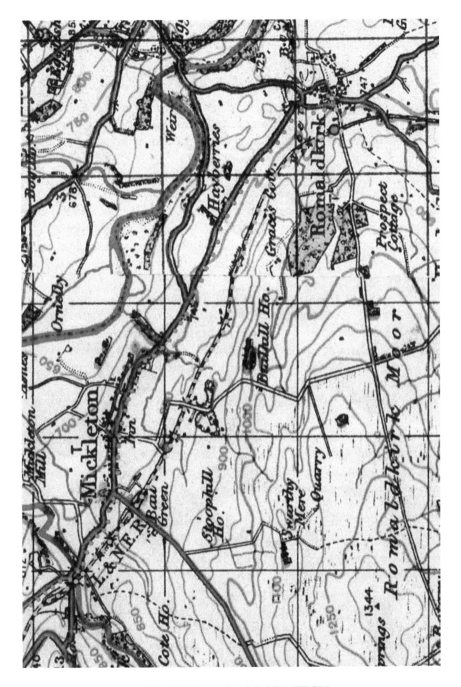

ROMALDKIRK – MICKLETON

DAY NO. 4/MAP NO.2 MICKLETON – MIDDLETON-IN-TEESDALE

Beyond Mickleton, the course of the railway crosses the valley of the River Lune via an impressive five-arched viaduct and on toward Middleton, which is now visible ahead. AW pronounced that the scenery rapidly deteriorated, industry having tainted it. The railway served not only passenger traffic but was also associated with the industry of the dale in moving stone from quarrying, and the line was extended beyond the passenger terminus at Middleton to the mines and the quarries at Park End and Crossthwaite.

The walk on the track bed ends at Lonton, where a short walk on the road takes us to a path descending to the river via Step Ends and onwards, following the access track to arrive at the road into the town. Turning right onto the road and crossing the bridge leads up Bridge Street into the town, the capital of the upper dale and former northern headquarters of the London Mining Company. It was they who were largely responsible for AW's derogatory view of the dale.

Lead-mining activity had been declining for many years as the price collapsed, which made extraction unviable, and it finally ceased in 1905. However, the quarries were still eating into the landscape and quarried stone was carried on the mineral railway to Middleton station and beyond. It was this extension that was reserved for AW's severest criticism in his description of how High Force deserved a poem, 'but it will never be written until the mine is abandoned and overgrown and the railway torn up'.

Of course, back in the day many local folk relied on the railway for a living. One such person was in fact Joyce Hughes, who followed her father to work on the railway during the war years at Middleton signal box. After the end of the war, road haulage became of greater importance and by 1951 the railway extension ceased to carry quarrying traffic. Soon after, AW had his wish when the mineral line was ripped up in 1952. Passenger services on the line down the dale from Middleton were withdrawn in 1964 and the track was lifted by 1967.

AW viewed Middleton-in-Teesdale as having a black mark for its enterprise and took the seemingly unfounded opinion that its inhabitants had, he feared, the minds of town-dwellers. The houses stood in ugly rows and that commercial gain from the earth was of greater import than the natural beauty. I had discovered more than once that the mention of AW did not generally gain positive responses.

The locals must however accept that, in 1940, it was reported that the river was all but devoid of salmon, so great was the residual pollution within the water; this should be compared with counts made sixty years earlier, when in excess of 100,000 salmon were fished. The years since the war have seen strides being made to see stocks being replenished and those efforts continue to this day, with recent moves toward a compulsory catch and release policy.

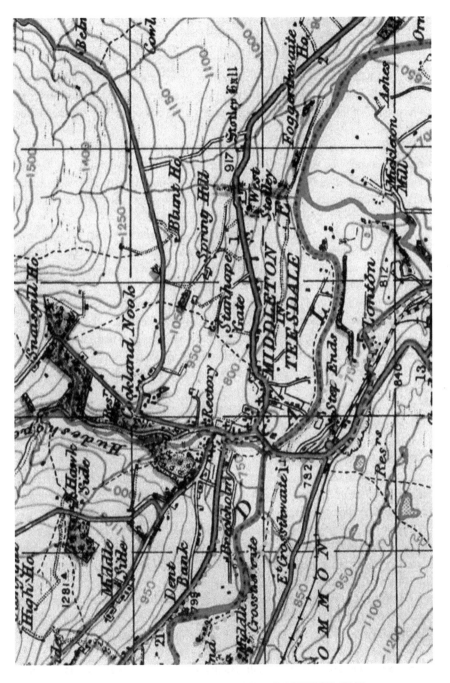

MICKLETON – MIDDLETON-IN-TEESDALE

DAY NO. 4/MAP NO.3 MIDDLETON-IN-TEESDALE –
BROADLEY'S GATE

Leaving Middleton, we join the Pennine Way again for a short while, following the southern bank of the river along a path that, in later years, had AW extolling its virtues in his recounting of the Pennine Way, considering it to be one of the best stretches of the whole walk.

His change of opinion was extreme from his comments within the Pennine Journey but it reflects generally the vast environmental improvements that have resulted in the area being well recognised as a botanists' dream. This fact was not missed by AW when, within his Pennine Way Companion, he mused that careful footwork was required to avoid treading on one of the many botanists crawling amongst the grasses.

Teesdale has seen a resurgence of natural fauna and flora and is recognised as an Area of Outstanding Natural Beauty. The AONB covers a huge area of the North Pennines, commencing beyond Middleton, and it is through the work of the groups existing within the partnership that the salmon stocks have seen growth in recent years.

We continue along the Pennine Way on the south side of the River Tees, with the desolate natural landscape of Swinhope Moor to the north and the equally desolate unnatural landscape of Crossthwaite Quarry to the south. We have a choice to make when we reach Scoberry Bridge, where the Pennine Way continues toward Wynch Bridge and Low Force. This is a fine alternative, but as the day's walk is already long enough I decided to cross at Scoberry.

A little way beyond Scoberry Bridge can be seen Holwick Lodge, owned by the Strathmore family, from which the Queen Mother was descended. Today the lodge is renowned for its shooting parties and has included Prince Charles among its guests.

The bridge itself dates from 1971, having been originally built late in the nineteenth century but closed after severe floods of 1942. Just before reaching a second footbridge crossing Bow Lee Beck, we turn left to make our way along the edge of the forestation of the Raby Estates and we follow the line of the wall all the way up to the B6277.

Crossing the road, a minor lane leads to the Bowlees Visitor Centre where there is a shop and a café; some sustenance might be wise before the slog up to Swinhope Head. Beyond the visitor centre, there is in fact a choice of ways, where a path can be followed to visit Gibson's Cave, named after an outlaw who was reputed to live beneath its overhanging rock ledges to escape the law. Whichever route is taken, they join again partway up Hare Hill, after which the path descends into the valley of Wester Beck before rising steeply at the other side on a line directly toward the white buildings that lie ahead, Broadley's Gate.

The path skirts around the right of the buildings and onto the access road and down to the Swinhope Moor road near Watson's Bridge.

MIDDLETON-IN-TEESDALE – BROADLEY'S GATE

DAY NO. 4/MAP NO.4 BROADLEY'S GATE – SWINHOPE HEAD

While it is unfortunate to be back on a hard road surface there is no practical alternative to the crossing of the moors other than to make use of the quiet and gated road. It is a pleasant enough route and must be viewed as being a means to an end; in other words, it will transport us from our morning's idyllic walking to an afternoon appointment with yet another beautiful valley route on a part of the Weardale Way.

A long, steady ascent lies before us, and after a distance of approximately 2 miles we reach the summit at Swinhope Head. The climb out of Teesdale begins to seem like an endless incline before the gate at the top is reached. The small consolation is that the verges comprise wide and springy grass and the ascent is rewarded by rearward views of the valley behind us.

As we leave Teesdale, we will have learned not to mention AW to the local folk, for his name is not held in high regard. His account of Teesdale told of scars that had been and still were being inflicted by industry. He wrote of fantastic shapes in the landscape that had been forged by man's insatiable desire for commercial gain. He had derided Middleton-in-Teesdale as a town with houses in ugly rows whose residents were not concerned with the beauty of their surrounds, their sole desire being to seek wealth that could be won from the earth.

It is, perhaps, only since AW's assassination that time has been allowed to heal the old wounds. In 1998 Teesdale had presented herself well with most of her injuries repaired. There is very little to see now of the dale's dark past and it is a shame that AW cannot return. The dale has a lot to commend it. Perhaps that poem can now be written.

The ruin of Flushiemere House creates some interest in an otherwise dreary landscape. The building lies derelict and has done so since 1949. It was a lodging house for Flushiemere baryte mine, which as late as 1941 was advertising for miners and labourers. Many mines ran along a similar basis where lodgings were provided from Monday to Friday with rudimentary accommodation afforded to the workers. The mine had been involved in lead extraction, but as that market decreased it concentrated on the mining of barytes from 1902 and later fluorspar, both of which found a variety of commercial uses.

After a long climb, the summit at Swinhope Head is reached and there is, at last, something to see ahead. Directly to the north, and our route down into Weardale, is the tributary valley of the Swinhope Burn. The map shows a path that cuts off a corner toward Swinhopehead House, but heed AW's account and do not attempt to follow this apparent short cut. I saw no trace of it on the ground and AW found it a quagmire and best avoided. 'Pass it by, if you are ever in Swinhope Head,' was his advice.

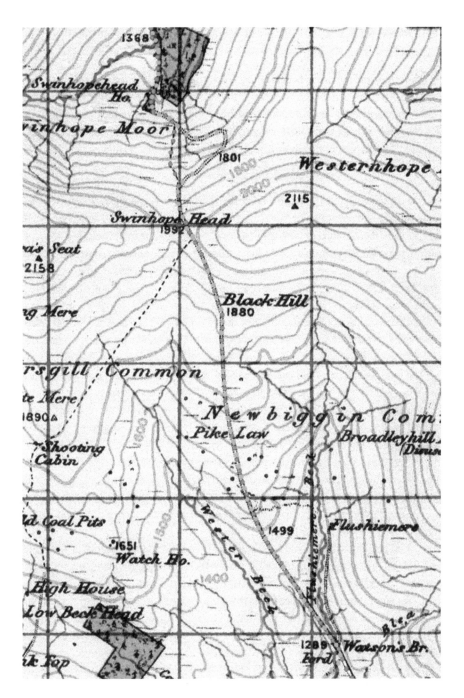

BROADLEY'S GATE – SWINHOPE HEAD

DAY NO. 4/MAP NO.5 SWINHOPE HEAD – WESTGATE

The minor and quiet road begins a long descent into the valley of the River Wear, following the western side of the Swinhope Burn tributary. To the west of Swinhopehead House (the deserted house where AW noted the washing on the line which was unlikely to dry as he walked in a clammy and damp mist), Swinhope Moor is the home to the Weardale Ski Club. Its two ski lifts provide access to thrill seekers in a north-east-facing natural amphitheatre but the après-ski looks a tad unexciting, the nearest habitation being Westgate, some 2 miles ahead.

Although road-walking is by now becoming tiresome, there is nothing by way of an alternative route and navigation remains straightforward, following the road northwards with little by way of civilisation until Swinside House is reached. The modern map shows that the area to the west of the house has the interesting title of 'Campmeeting Allotment'.

The title of these meadows relates back the early days of the Methodism in Weardale. The movement had suffered persecution over many years but was beginning to be accepted by the establishment and had found a home in the northern dales. Although the first chapel in Westgate was not completed until 1824, the previous year had seen a mass al fresco gathering, with over 200 attending the camp at what is still known as 'Campmeeting Allotment'.

The road begins to descend into the valley and at a crossroads a sign indicates our target, Westgate, via a ford. As we have kept our feet dry thus far it would be sad if we now had to wade our way into the village. Thankfully, a little way beyond the remnants of the railway bridge abutments, there is a footbridge over the river and we proceed into what appears to be a caravan site.

Westgate is yet another village that had enjoyed a railway link back in 1938, having been reached by the Bishop Auckland and Weardale Railway as late as 1895. The line had been built in sections up the dale generally to reach sites of industry, but as the various sites fell into decline then so did the line, which ceased to carry passengers in 1953 and finally closed in 1968.

The origin of the village name is derived from back in the day when much of Weardale was forested and in the ownership of the Prince Bishops. Westgate marked the western boundary of the forest with Eastgate at the eastern edge.

In Westgate, we join the Weardale Way for a short distance as we turn north from Front Street toward an area of Westgate known as High Town. Proceeding up Scutterhill Bank, where the Weardale Way turns eastward at a stile, we follow the path to the left and head north toward High Mill, which was one of two corn mills serving the village in days long gone when mining swelled the local population. Beyond High Mill the path continues north into Slit Wood as it follows Middlehope Burn.

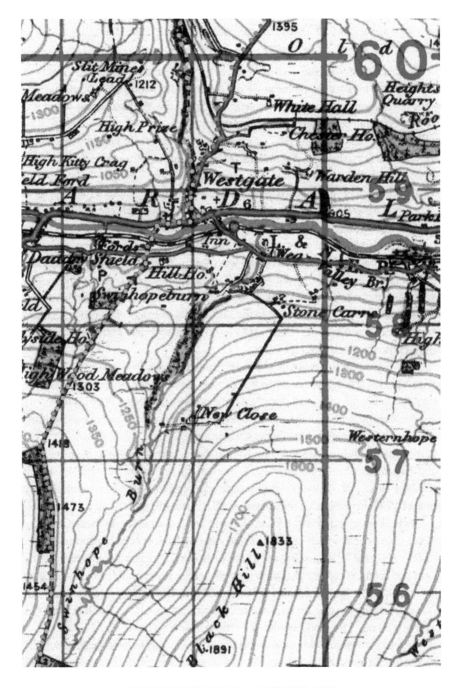

SWINHOPE HEAD – WESTGATE

DAY NO. 4/MAP NO.6 WESTGATE – ROOKHOPE

We could leave Westgate via the Weardale Way and follow the route all the way to Rookhope, but to do so would mean we are more removed from AW's route and also would result in our not savouring this particularly pleasing walk through Slit Wood and along the delightful banks of the Middlehope Burn.

The path beyond High Mill passes a series of terraced waterfalls, formed where harder sandstone overlies softer shale. It then leads into lead mining country, evidenced by a selection of ruined buildings and a sense of an unnatural landscape. The valley is littered with old mines, the first of which, Slit (or Slitt) mine, has enough of its infrastructure in place to give a sense of the industry that existed here in the extraction of lead. The North Pennines was globally recognised as one of the major lead-producing areas.

The level land adjacent to the burn is an area known as the washing floor, where ore was extracted from the mined material. The water for this was provided from the millpond, which is sited to the west of the watercourse. The shaft for the mine is on the other side of the stream and comprises a vertical shaft, some 200 metres deep, which would have been accessed by a series of ladders. Next to the shaft are the remnants of a huge waterwheel assembly and engine housing, which would be driven by the water from the millpond to keep the mine free from flooding.

There is much to be admired in the sheer scale of industry in this valley and there is something spectral in the ethereal remains from those days long ago. There was not just one mine; continuing the walk northwards we come across Middlehope Shield followed by High Middlehope mines. All the mines would have been connected by a mineral railway, hauled by ponies, carrying lead ore to the smelting mill.

At High Middlehope, we leave the burn to follow a track to join an unmade road, which takes an unnaturally straight course to connect with a minor metalled road leading up to Scarsike Head. Although an unwelcome return to macadam, walking through the history lesson of Middlehope Burn has rendered it a small price to pay.

Descending beyond Scarsike Head, the road walking ends at Lintzgarth Common, where a choice of paths leads easterly with the valley of the Rookhope Burn opening up. It is to Rookhope that we are heading and it is here that I would suggest that an overnight stop is arranged, for the remaining sections of the walk to Blanchland would be best undertaken after rest. The other benefit of resting at Rookhope is that as it lies on the recognised Coast to Coast cycleway there is a greater choice of accommodation, whereas Blanchland has less variety on offer. The Rookhope Inn is a delightful watering hole.

The final 2 miles to Rookhope is a gradual descent across fields until finally arriving at a footbridge that leads into the village.

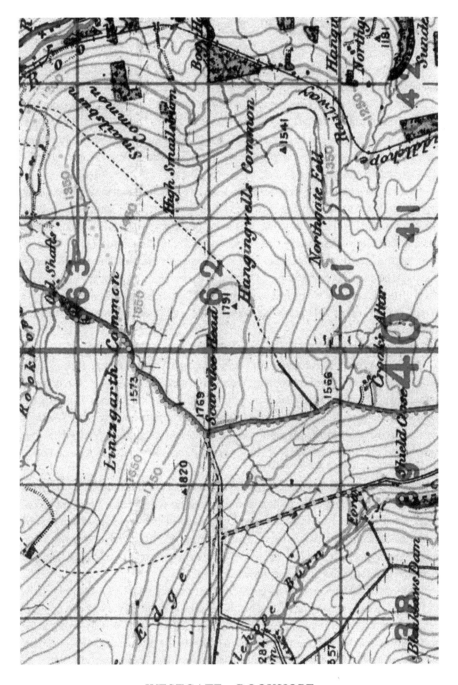

WESTGATE – ROOKHOPE

DAY NO. 4/MAP NO.7 ROOKHOPE – BOLT'S LAW

Rookhope is another village steeped in the history of lead mining and has a number of claims to fame. The first was referred to by AW in his account, where he related the story of the tale of the Border Reivers coming into the dale to plunder livestock. AW recounted that the ballad relating this tale was by 'Scott or somebody'. Unusually for AW he was incorrect, as the fable refers to an event long before Scott was born, with the Rookhope men driving out the northerners empty-handed. There is no accreditation for the author but Scott it certainly was not.

Rookhope's other claims are to be discovered as we start the ascent toward Bolt's Law, proceeding up the track north-east from the village. We have already seem how, in 1938, when AW made his trek in the northern Pennines, he did so in the shadow of one literary giant, J. B. Priestley who, among other works, had told of his 'English Journey'. At Rookhope, another noted writer and poet, W. H. Auden, later recalled how it was that at Rookhope he had first became aware of himself as a poet during a visit at just twelve years old in 1919. He and AW were of very similar ages, having been born just five weeks apart in early 1907. Auden's 1941 poem 'New Year Letter'is a lengthy philosophical poem that includes the words:

"There in Rookhope I was first aware of Self and Not-Self, Death and Dread"

The same poem makes reference to Bolt's Law, which brings us to the next claim to fame. Back in the mid-nineteenth century, the north Pennine region was of such importance in the mining of lead that the owners were willing to go to great lengths and sizable expense to increase its output. This extended to the construction of a railway network from workings between Rookhope and Blanchland to connect to the smelting mills of Weardale. This railway also extended southwards of Rookhope via Smailsburn and Northgate and on to Scuttershill above Westgate.

Reference to the modern maps shows the vast extent of this railway system, which was of standard gauge and was the highest such gauge ever constructed in England as it contoured around Bolt's Law. The Bolt Law incline was closed in 1941, leaving the Rookhope works cut off from the network, a problem which was solved by the construction of an aerial ropeway to Eastgate. The ropeway is now long gone and what remains are just memories in the scars that this former life has left behind.

As the rail trackway curves to the east, our route branches off north toward Bolt's Law, and we will quickly appreciate walking in this desolate landscape at the start of a new day rather than attempting it as the last stage of an already long day's trek. At a crossroads in the path, our way is to head off north-easterly on a bridle path on a gradual descent, on a bearing between the two small stretches of water that lie about one kilometre ahead.

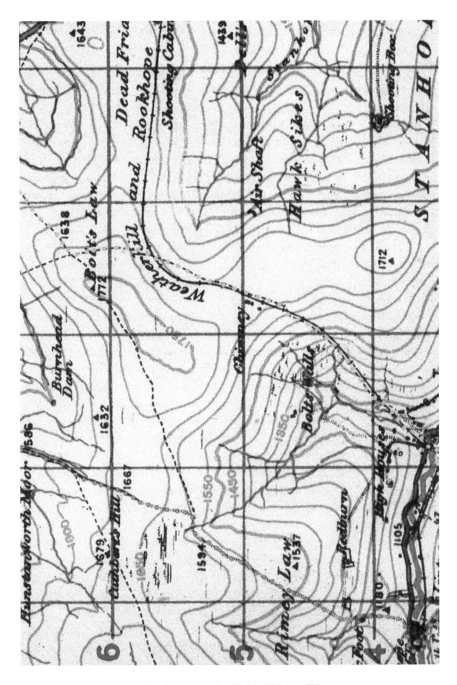

ROOKHOPE – BOLT'S LAW

DAY NO. 4/MAP NO.8 BOLT'S LAW – BLANCHLAND

If you have decided to follow AW's stopover, then this is the last section of a very long day; if you have taken my advice then the legs will be fresh to enjoy the history that these hills exude.

Blanchland lies just 3 miles down in the valley ahead, where a village in which time has stood still since the days when it developed around the monks of the abbey awaits. There is a story that, many years ago, the monks became aware of a Scottish raiding party seeking to plunder the abbey and they prayed for deliverance. Their prayers appeared to have been answered when a thick mist descended and prevented the raiders from finding the village. It is said that the raiders were on the hills to the south when the monks, in celebration of their salvation, rang the church bells as in glory to God.

The monks don't seem to have bargained on the raiders hearing the bells and following the sound to find the abbey. The hill to the right as we proceed north-east is thought to be the hill from where the raiders turned about – the hill is still known as Dead Friars Hill for obvious reasons.

Although the suggested route takes us directly to the minor road, Meadows Edge, as it crosses the wild heather moors, there is an alternative to find a path to Sikehead Dam. With the chimney at the southern end of the dam as our guide, we then cross the dam until a path follows the disused flue, the arched structure which is exposed in places and can be seen. When in use, the flue carried toxic fumes to be released away from the smelting plant. Residues of the fumes would be collected as a high-quality byproduct on the sides of the flue and once a year or so some poor soul would work the length of the flue to extract the material in an environment that would be more hazardous than the mine itself.

Just before the flue turns north-west, a track leads us away to join the road, which we follow only for a short distance before branching off again on the final stretch. Following this bridle path as far as 970480, we then follow a boundary wall across Buckshott Fell until we rejoin macadam at a sharp corner. Heading downhill here takes us to Bridge End and on into Blanchland.

As we follow the road, we enter Northumberland and find ourselves in the county that contains the target of our venture, the Wall. As we cross the River Derwent, it is easy to see why AW waxed lyrical about Blanchland as it nestles on the valley floor. Were it not for the modern street furniture there is nothing that visually separates the view before us from the Blanchland that AW would have entered in 1938.

One of the main reasons to have shortened Day 4 to end at Rookhope is that for those looking for overnight accommodation at Blanchland, with the exception of the Lord Crewe Arms, there is little by way of guesthouses.

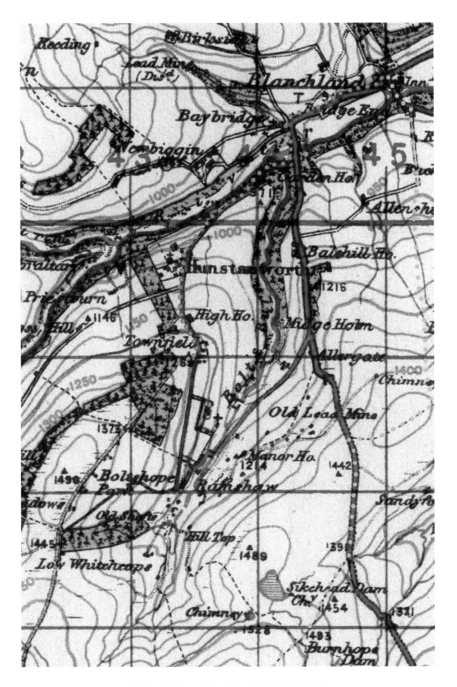

BOLT'S LAW – BLANCHLAND

DAY NO. 5

BLANCHLAND TO HEXHAM

DAY NO. 5

BLANCHLAND TO HEXHAM

If the walk is undertaken as AW suggested, then Day 5 is a very short 10 miles, and even if the day begins at Rookhope it is still the shortest walking day so far in our journey. The route from Blanchland climbs out of the Derwent valley and over Blanchland Moor before entering the parish of Hexham Low Quarter and descending to West Dipton Burn before ascending again to Yarridge Hill and down into Hexham itself.

Leg	From:	To:
5 – 1	Blanchland	Acton Fell
5 – 2	Acton Fell	Dye House
5 – 3	Dye House	Plover Hill
5 – 4	Plover HIll	Hexham

Once we have left Blanchland there is little by way of opportunity to buy provisions before reaching Hexham other than the stop at the delightful Dipton Mill Inn. The route also takes in the last of the lead-mining evidence at the Dukesfield smelting mill, recently renovated. We will revisit further lead-mining remnants but only as we near Alston at the end of Day 7.

The maps required for the day will depend upon the chosen starting point. Assuming that a start is made at Rookhope then two maps will be needed, the first from the Ordnance Survey 'Explorer' range:

307   Consett and Derwent Reservoir

From Blanchland onwards, the following map is required form the OS 'Outdoor Leisure' series:

OL43   Hadrian's Wall (Haltwhistle & Hexham)

The end of the day's walking sees us approaching Hexham via busy suburban roads so take care in walking amongst traffic from Hexham Racecourse down into the town itself.

The choice of overnight stops will impact on the distances to be covered:

Rookhope–Hexham   17 miles allow 7 hours
Blanchland–Hexham   12 miles allow 5 hours

DAY NO. 5/MAP NO.1 BLANCHLAND – ACTON FELL

AW noted that the village of Blanchland had an appearance of time having stood still and having an air of a military encampment where a suit of armour would be more the correct style of dress. This observation was incorrect and the village owes its initial development to the white monks of the twelfth century. It was they who suffered at the hands of the raiders and also the Dissolution during the reign of Henry VIII.

The modern appearance of the village is the result of more recent history. Lord Crewe had become the owner of the village and on his death a trust was established through his will; after a long period of decay and dereliction, in the 1750s the trustees of the Lord Crewe Estate oversaw the building of the village very much as it is seen today. The abbey had fallen into disrepair and much of the new model village was built from stone salvaged from the ruins.

There is good reason for the village appearing as if time has stood still, and it relates to the nature of property tenures. The properties are not owned freehold by the occupants, instead the freeholder is the trustees of the estate and any development has to be sanctioned by them before it will be allowed. I learned from discussions in 1998 that strict interpretation of these conditions had extended to TV aerials and satellite dishes not being allowed and even the construction of a greenhouse requiring approval. It is also of note that all the dwellings have painted external timberwork of similar colour to a shade agreed by the trustees.

As far as possible, the street furniture is kept to a minimum and even street lighting is by way of lamps affixed to the buildings themselves rather than via freestanding lamp standards. The maintaining of services in such an 'olde-worlde' manner has had its downsides, one of which must have been that it was only in the mid-1960s that each property was connected to mains sewerage. Prior to that, effluent was removed from earth closets with the contents being collected by horse and cart each night.

We leave Blanchland via the road to the left of the White Monk Tearooms, formerly the schoolhouse until it, like several previous, succumbed to falling numbers and closed in 1981. A short way up this road, the second property on the left was known as 'The Surgery' (as it still was when I stayed in 1998, when it was a guesthouse, as its last paying guest, the landlady due to take up a post at the nearby Slaley Hall) because it doubled as a surgery for the visiting doctor.

The minor road leads out of the village and past the huge car park, which serves to show how busy the village can become at peak times. It proceeds via a delightful narrow single-track lane uphill to Shildon. Here the long-abandoned lead mine workings are surrounded by evidence of old dwellings that was the major habitation prior to the eighteenth-century rebuilding of Blanchland itself.

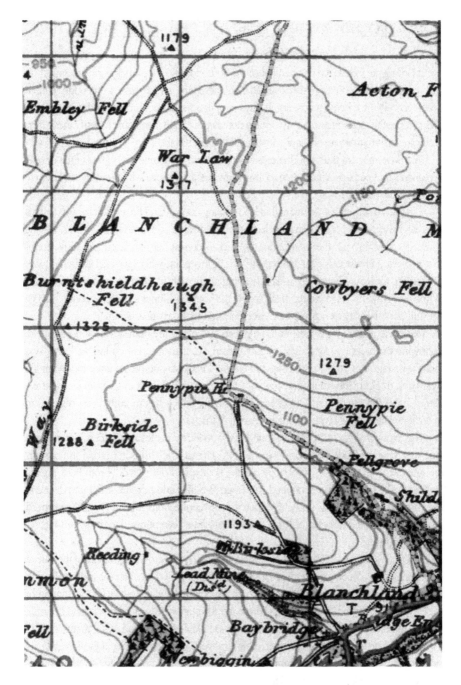

BLANCHLAND – ACTON FELL

DAY NO. 5/MAP NO.2 ACTON FELL – DYE HOUSE

At Pennypie House we proceed left of the house to follow the track northwards and we are now on an old drovers' road over Blanchland Moor, which passes this oddly named house, so called for being a hostelry in days long ago for passing miners and carriers, with pies presumably costing one penny! I have not unequivocally been able to ratify these facts but I can confirm that pies are sadly not available these days!

The drovers' road tracks north across the moorland landscape and there is little of note hereabouts and perhaps anticipation of tomorrow's acquaintance with the wall can begin to creep into our thoughts.

It is easy to forget that we are still in lead-mining country and the track itself was once a busy highway with ponies carrying lead ore northwards to the smelting works that lie ahead. Passing through the forestation, the track becomes hard-surfaced and turns north-east towards a crossroads near Holly Hill. It is at this point where we part company with AW again, for he continued north-east, heading all the way to Hexham on metalled roads. While following his route would mean seeing the house at Linnel's Bridge, about which he was full of praise, it does not merit the decidedly dangerous road-walking.

Our route instead turns west at the junction and along the narrow lane to Dukesfield. Following the quiet byway to Middle Dukesfield, we then fork left on the track that was many years ago the Lead Road, passed Dukesfield Hall, staying on the track following the west bank of Hall Burn to its junction with Devil's Water. It is at this confluence that we come across the remains of Dukesfield Smelt Mill, which has recently been restored to maintain what is left of its grand but eerie arched structure.

The remains of the mill are to be found in a wooded ravine known, with something of a clue, as Furnace Wood. This was once one of the largest smelt mills in Europe and ore was brought from as far away as Rookhope, via the Pennypie drovers' road. From here, pigs of lead would be taken via pony on the Lead Road to Slaley and beyond. It fell into disuse in the mid-nineteenth century, probably when railway connections around Rookhope proved more efficient in the carrying of lead ore, and has since been allowed to decay until its recent restoration.

It is likely that the mill would use similar ventilation flues to the remnants of the flue at Sikehead Mill on the moors south of Blanchland. Leadpipe Hill, which we walked close to through the forest, was very likely so called because it formed the outlet for the venting of the toxic fumes for the smelting long before the forestation was planted. Beyond the mill, we turn left on the road and make our way over the Devil's Water and uphill to turn right at a junction toward the hamlet of Juniper. A little way beyond Dye House, at the corner in the lane, a path leads north before crossing an unmade track and continuing. As we head towards Smelting Syke, keep the wall to the right.

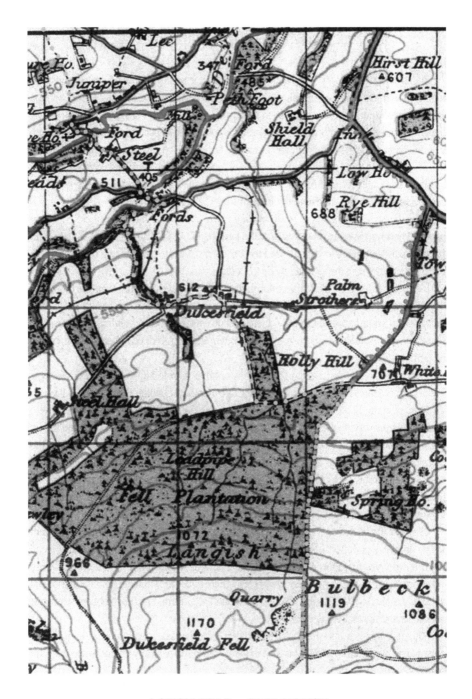

ACTON FELL – DYE HOUSE

DAY NO. 5/MAP NO.3 DYE HOUSE – PLOVER HILL

We are now walking in the Hexham Low Quarter parish and, although we have left behind the remnants of lead mining, we are now in an area whose history of habitation dates back to medieval times. One such settlement, the hamlet of Ordley, lies a short way along the road east of Juniper and was classed as a large town back in the seventeenth century. The area has a history of feudal skirmishes and there are several properties within the vicinity that were built with an emphasis on defence. Various examples of these fortified buildings particular to northern Britain, known as bastles, can be found throughout Northumberland and there are several in Hexham Low Quarter.

Having crossed the track, the path leading north follows the line of the field boundary through Blackhall Wood and on towards the farm buildings at Smelting Syke. It turns right just before the buildings to join the road for a short distance before crossing the timber stile and following the path through the fields to Dotland Park.

Dotland Park is a Grade II listed farmhouse and is a short distance from the hamlet of Dotland, which is noted on the modern map as being the site of a medieval village. It is unclear as to what happened to the settlement but what had been a settlement of approximately twenty households in the sixteenth century had been reduced over the centuries to the farm that is left today.

The access track from Dotland Park leads north and on to Hill Road, which we cross onto a narrow lane leading downhill to the bridge over West Dipton Burn and a chance for refreshment at the Dipton Mill Inn. In the seventeenth and eighteenth centuries, there were many local inns serving the drovers of Hexhamshire but The Dipton is the only one left. In part it owes its survival to the owner having established Hexhamshire Brewery. The characterful logo for the brews comprises an image of a barrel being carried by two men, and is based on a Thomas Bewick engraving. It was only after the brewery was set up in 1992 that an elderly local advised that the image was actually of urine being carried to the tannery at Hexham in years gone by.

Crossing the bridge over the water, our route leads along the northern bank of the burn before finding a path north out of the steep wooded valley until breaking out into Peterel Field. If we were to continue west along the burn we would arrive at Queens Cave, so called because it is said that Queen Margaret hid here after the Battle of Hexham in the final battle of the Wars of the Roses, having been found at Queens Letch by robbers who took pity on her and agreed to hide her.

Although this is a fine story, it is generally considered completely untrue, as it is now known that by the time of the battle Margaret was already safely many miles away in France.

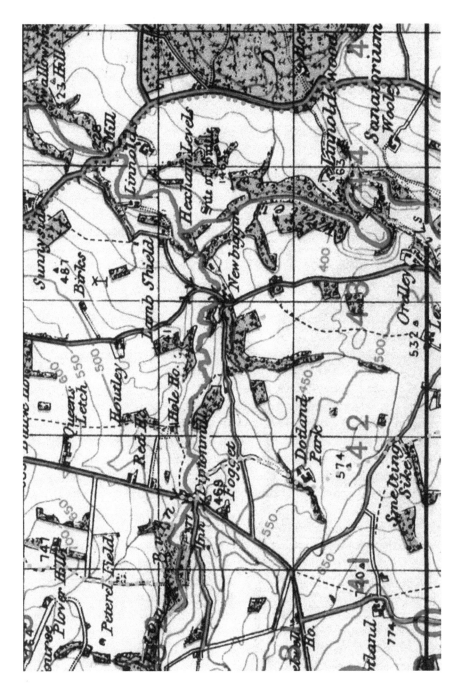

DYE HOUSE – PLOVER HILL

DAY NO. 5/MAP NO.4 PLOVER HILL – HEXHAM

To the west of Plover Hill is Hexham Racecourse, Northumberland's only surviving racecourse. Although racing on the site has a long history, the present infrastructure dates from a layout started in 1890. Racing has continued here ever since, aside from its requisition by the military as an ammunition store for the duration of the Second World War, starting the year after AW's visit. The path meets the Yarridge Road at Rising Sun Farm and proceeds across the road down Causey Hill Road, descending into the town lying ahead. AW had noted in his account that there were many new houses being built and it is evident from comparing the old map with the new that urban sprawl has swallowed up much of what would have been greenbelt. Contrasted with the modern suburbia, in 1938 Causey Hill Road, was largely rural along its length to where it joins Allendale Road.

At this spot, the local paper, the Hexham Courant, reported a very sad coincidence just a matter of days before AW's visit to the town. Two days' walking will see us arrive in the Cumbrian town of Alston but just prior to AW being at Hexham a tragedy occured that linked the two towns. At the bottom of Causey Hill Road the vicar of Alston, Revd Wynne Owen, had been driving west on Allendale Road when he lost control and skidded into the wall, dying at the scene.

Turning right, the route is now all on urban roads into the centre of Hexham, turning left into Beaumont Street towards the abbey. Passing along Beaumont Street, the Queens Hall on the right is where AW went to see the film The Housemaster to get himself away from his cold lodgings at the Abbey Tearoom. There is now no trace of the tearoom but perhaps more pleasant accommodation can be found in any case. A little way down Market Street is to be found the Heart of All England public house, now an upmarket eatery. The same name is also given to the Hexham Racecourse premier steeplechase cup, the meeting of which is held each May. The reference to the heart of all England is reputed to have derived from James I who, on travelling south in 1603, declared that 'verily this is the Heart of all England'.

While his proclamation was somewhat geographically questionable, the sentiment behind it has been happily adopted by the town. When I visited, the public house was a fine hostelry in which good standard fare could be found. The Heart of All England steeplechase has been run since 1907, when the local tradesmen presented the cup. The race meeting has taken place each year since with the exception of the war years.

In 1938, the European negotiations between Chamberlain and Hitler were ongoing and as AW sat in the cinema and then walked the streets, the discussions in Germany had ended with the Munich Agreement, with Chamberlain returning triumphant.

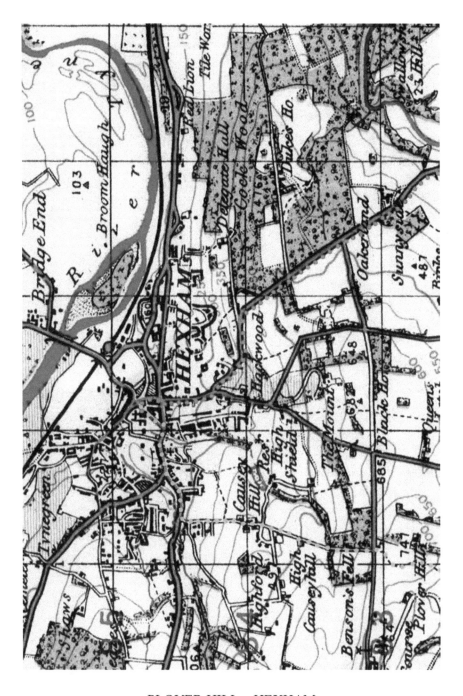

PLOVER HILL – HEXHAM

DAY NO. 6

HEXHAM TO HALTWHISTLE

DAY NO. 6

HEXHAM TO HALTWHISTLE

Today is the culmination of the previous five days' labours as we finally reach the Roman Wall. We will walk along what is without doubt the best stretches of its remains. During the day's walk, we will achieve half-distance and will reach the most northerly point of our excursion. We will join the Hadrian's Wall National Trail on reaching the wall and, for part of the day, join once again with the Pennine Way.

The route starts as a road walk leaving Hexham, then heading north on quiet byways via Warden before following the wall west for approximately 10 miles before turning south for Haltwhistle. It is feasible to find accommodation other than at Haltwhistle but this choice would depend on how much you wish to experience of AW's original walk.

Along the way we will encounter other fascinating aspects of the history hereabouts, including the early days of the Boy Scout movement and the strange origin of the naming of a hamlet with two names. We will even come across a more recent history linked to a Hollywood blockbuster.

The day is split into six legs and should not provide any difficulties in navigation.

Leg	From:	To:
6 – 1	Hexham	Warden
6 – 2	Warden	Walwick Fell
6 – 3	Walwick Fell	Milestone 26
6 – 4	Milestone 26	Housesteads
6 – 5	Housesteads	Twice Brewed
6 – 6	Twice Brewed	Haltwhistle

The total day's walk is approximately 22 miles with limited scope for refreshment stops other than the worthwhile diversion to the Housesteads Visitor Centre. In terms of alternative overnight accommodation (to avoid the 2 mile road walk), the Twice Brewed Inn or the Once Brewed youth hostel might suffice but this would lengthen Day 7. The choice is yours, but I personally wanted to see if the town that AW thought so little of has more modern redeeming facets that would alter his opinion.

The day's walking is contained on one map from the Ordnance Survey 'Outdoor Leisure' series:

      OL43   Hadrian's Wall (Haltwhistle & Hexham)

The final part of the walking for the day descends into Haltwhistle along the narrow road, Shield Hill, which winds its way from the B6318 down into the town. Take care on this road for it is without pavements for much of its length.

The total time taken for the day will depend upon how much of a worthy distraction Hadrian's Wall proves to be and also if a diversion is made to the visitor centre at Housesteads. I suggest that 10 hours should be allowed

Horton in Ribblesdale church

DAY NO. 6/MAP NO.1 HEXHAM – WARDEN

It is unlikely that we will wake up to such momentous news as AW had awoken to during his stay in Hexham on that last day of September in 1938. As he arose, he did so to the newspaper stands declaring that the country had averted war and that Neville Chamberlain had secured 'peace for our time' at Munich. Chamberlain returned to England and made his infamous 'I have in my hand a piece of paper' speech that within a year was to haunt him and see him judged as a weak leader forevermore.

AW had been relieved by this news and was elated at the prospect of what the day held in store. He made an interesting insight into his self-perception in his narrative when he wrote that he had wished that all his friends could join him in his bed – he went on to write 'alas, there would be ample room'. He made no further reference to such matters but this sentiment would suggest that, even though he seemed to be something of a wag at work, he perceived himself as more of a loner.

Retracing his route, we leave the town via Market Street, passing the 'Heart of All England' public house, joining Eilansgate and following it to join the B6531 and on to its junction with the A69. These road numberings that we rely on are not to be found on any of the old maps that AW used for his journey. Although the Ministry of Transport, formed in 1919, had been charged with establishing a system of road classification it was some years before the first numbering appeared on road atlases and OS maps.

Road classification had not been included on the Ordnance Survey maps, although it should also be noted that some details throughout the 1930s were deliberately omitted from OS maps in the interests of national security.

After carefully crossing the major trunk road, a quiet road leads toward West Boat and the bridge over the River South Tyne into the hamlet of Bridge End. There used to be a ferry crossing at this point with an inn at either side. The Boatside Inn remains on the north bank but the West Boat Inn is long gone. It is referred in an article in the Hexham Courant during 1938 in a story relating to the replacement of a flood marker stone which had vanished some time earlier. The article confirmed that the inn had largely disappeared, having been closed for some years. To the left of the bridge parapet on the south bank is a building that was the toll house to the original suspension bridge across the river. That bridge collapsed in 1877 and the current stone bridge was built in 1903.

Once across the bridge, our route is to turn right at the Boatside Inn onto the quiet lane that leads to the village of Warden. Warden Church, and especially its tower, which had attracted AW's attention for its lack of a clock, is at least partly built of stone believed to have been lifted from the Wall.

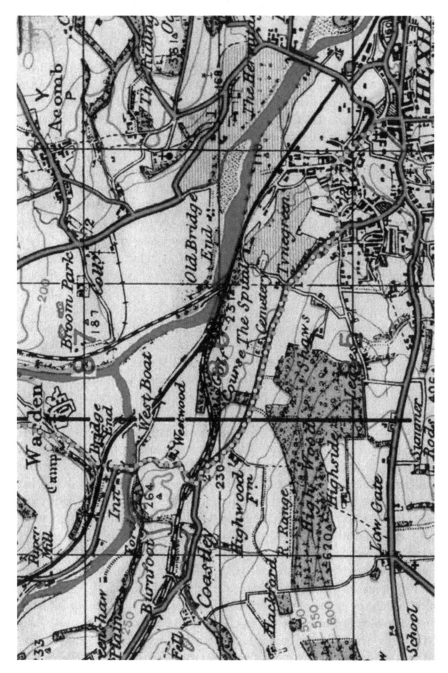

HEXHAM – WARDEN

DAY NO. 6/MAP NO.2 WARDEN – WALWICK FELL

The church at Warden is the first of many examples of architecture close to the wall that has benefitted from the work of Roman stone masons. Prior to continuing north and leaving Warden, a small deviation will take us a short way along the access road to Warden Church, where there are three gravestones dated 1862 just inside the lych gate. Peculiar to these stones is that they have hooped iron bars fitted as a precaution against body-snatchers, it being rife at the time for bodies to be dug up and stolen, then sold and used for medical research.

The lane leading northwards from Warden, Homer's Lane, provides us with the day's final mile or so of walking along a surfaced road. At the junction at Walwick Grange, we finally will have grass under our feet as we turn west to follow the track to the farm at Park Shield. As much as I wish to retrace AW's route, it is preferable to be off the hard macadam. AW had continued on to the Roman fort at Chesters; I conclude that Chesters can be visited on a separate occasion by car and also the walk uphill west from Walwick along the line of the wall is not ideal, the wall itself being buried under the road.

There is another reason to wish to visit Park Shield; to see the site of the first official scout camp after the inauguration of the Scouts Movement. What we now take for granted with all scout and guide packs had not happened prior to 1908, when a group of thirty 'nominated' boys took part in the first official camp. The nominations were generated via voting slips available in the The Scout magazine, which must have helped boost sales of what was a new publication in April 1908. By the time of the announcement of the lucky winners, the most votes cast for one of the thirty was 29,000 and was generally seen as a somewhat cynical ploy to increase sales.

The Humhaugh Camp, as it was known, took place over two weeks, starting in late August. Leaving Park Shield, we follow the access track and join the minor road heading north. The actual site of the camp was in the field to the left of the road and the site is referred to in a Hexham Courant article in 1938, which related the story of how the local scouts had visited the memorial erected to the 1908 camp. The memorial was erected in 1929 as a cairn at the northern end of the campsite in the Carr Edge Plantation, and commemorated the events of 1908.

Baden-Powell attended the camp himself and wrote in his diary of the 'views of the mighty Roman wall', but it is recorded that this entry was actually written while he was sitting on higher ground north of the plantation. It is only here that the wall first becomes visible on our trek. A short distance beyond the campsite, a path leads off towards Walwick Fell, passing the remains of an even earlier encampment. This camp is of Roman origin, acting as a service station while the wall itself was being constructed. This station is not shown on the AW map and we will see other examples of discoveries that have only been identified after AW's visit.

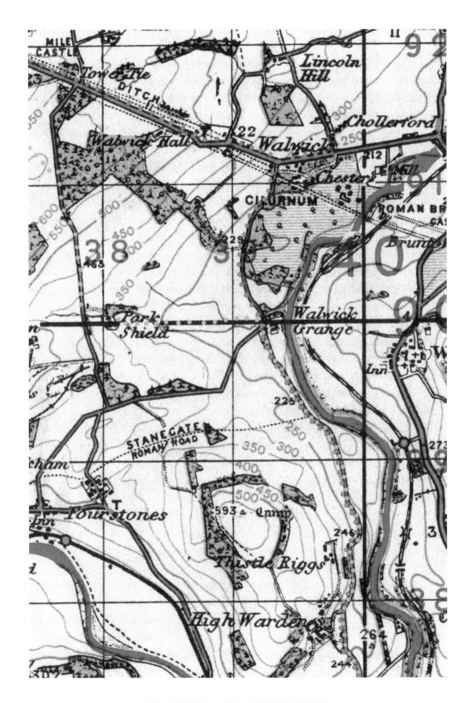

WARDEN – WALWICK FELL

DAY NO. 6/MAP NO.3 WALWICK FELL – MILESTONE 26

There is plenty of printed material relating to Hadrian's Wall, so it isn't the aim of this account to provide details of its construction other than to briefly outline its four principal elements. The line of the wall itself in the main is followed by an excavated ditch immediately to the north, with a wider dished excavation to the south known as the Vallum. Generally running between the Vallum and the wall is a military roadway built to provide speed of transport for goods and soldiers.

Our first encounter with the wall is in our descent from Walwick Fell, which drops to meet the B6318, known as the 'Military Road', which is not to be confused with the military way described above. Under the direction of General Wade, it was one of many such roads built to help maintain control of those who were involved in the Jacobite rebellions of 1715 and 1745. It is, though, a sad fact that this section of the wall provided both the line and much of the materials for the building of the road, with the result that large parts of the wall have been significantly reduced, in some places leaving next to no evidence of the wall itself. Wade's road does in part follow the line of the Vallum, but even where this is the case the wall's height and majesty have been greatly reduced after having had its walling stones salvaged by the eighteenth-century military.

We cross the B6318 and for few yards proceed along the minor road to a stile on the left. Where we join the course of the wall, we do so at a point where there remains a very clear line of masonry near to Black Carts Farm. At the gap in the wall's visible remains, known as Hen Gap, we cross the stile heading west toward Limestone Bank and are now walking on the Hadrian's Wall Path National Trail.

Limestone Bank is memorable in our passing for a number of reasons. It represents half-distance and also the most northerly point in our travels. It also provides the first chance to enjoy the wall where the Roman military way can be seen and where there is sufficient distance between the wall and the road to gain a sense of the remoteness of our position.

The manual effort needed to construct the ditch is abundantly clear where the wall bends. The base rock hereabouts is hard basalt and the rock has been split to allow excavation using wedges. On the summit the Roman quarrymen gave up, and the holes where the wedges would have been inserted can still be seen.

Continuing west along the trail, passing Carrawbrough Farm, we soon arrive at another example of how the wall continues to give up its secrets. At the Roman fort Brocolitia, a short diversion will take us to the site of a temple only discovered in 1949. Mithraeum, as marked on the new map, is not shown on AW's map for it was to be another eleven years before it would be unearthed. The summer of 1949 was particularly dry and the usually boggy ground dried and contracted, allowing the temple's three altars to be exposed and fully excavated in 1950.

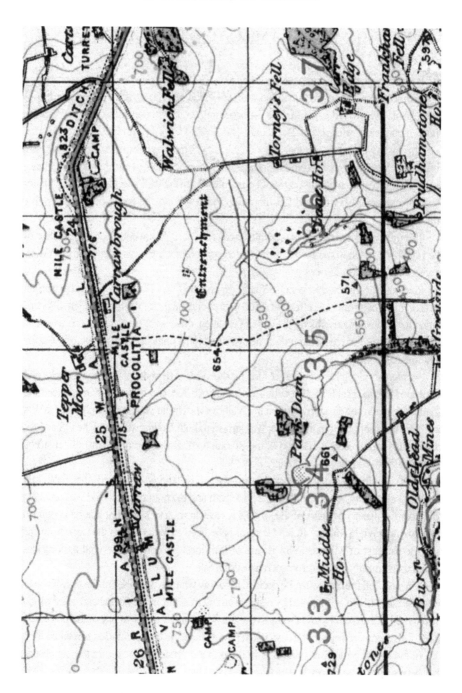

WALWICK FELL – MILESTONE 26

DAY NO. 6/MAP NO.4 MILESTONE 26 – HOUSESTEADS

References to the old and new maps appear to show discrepancies as to the numbering of the milecastles. When we joined the wall and made our way to the milecastle at Limestone Bank, we arrived at Milecastle 30 according to the modern map, but AW's map shows a numerical reference of 24.

The answer lies in the fact that although the old OS map shows milecastles, the number referencing does not relate to the milecastles but to milestones along the Wade Military Road. This is best seen on this section of our walk where the wall's castles and the Military Road are separated but the old OS map numbering follows the road and not the wall's milecastles.

The milecastle numbering is generally credited to J. Collingwood Bruce, the author of the Handbook to the Roman Wall, the abridged version of which was referred to by AW as having fired his enthusiasm.

Each of the milecastles is not actually separated by an 'English' mile; the Roman measurement of a mile was closer to 1,500 metres and each one comprised a gated fortification for troops stationed along the wall. In addition, there were two smaller constructions known as turrets between each milecastle, assumed to be manned by a section of the adjacent milecastle troops.

At intervals along the wall, larger forts provided more permanent military barracks and associated service buildings. Brocolitia was one such fort and has already evidenced the continuing nature of discovery where the Mithraeum temple was found only after AW's trek. The fort itself, back in the 1930s, was known to both Collingwood and the OS as Procolitia but a more recent translation of the Roman texts show its name as most likely to be the name shown on the modern maps.

Since joining the national trail, our way has largely followed the road but, finally, a short way beyond Milestone 27, the path and the road bifurcate and we can begin to savour the peace and quiet of the wall. It is clear from AW's account that he continued to follow the Wade Military Road. He must have lived to regret this as the walk from the turret to the east of Milecastle 34 is one of the finest sections of the wall as it strides across the summit of the escarpment of the Whin Sill.

AW only left the road when he decided to follow what he described as the easy slope to Housesteads, only to be thwarted by a sign warning of a bull in the field ahead, after which he returned to the road. He did then arrive at the pedestrian entrance to one of the best excavated forts along the wall. In the days when he was here, the farmer acted as caretaker, long before the visitor centre was built. It is well worth a diversion to the centre to help absorb the sheer scope of the history in which we find ourselves.

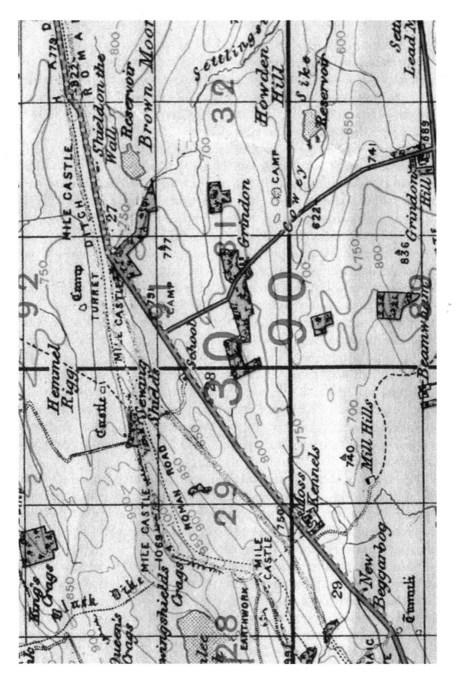

MILESTONE 26 – HOUSESTEADS

DAY NO. 6/MAP NO.5 HOUSESTEADS – TWICE BREWED

Housesteads, known by the Romans as Vercovicium, translating as 'Place of the effective fighters', is the best known and most visited of the forts along the wall. It has also been subject of a name change, for on the map AW was using it was noted as Borcovicium, and it was indeed noted in the Spectator in January 1931 by that name when it was reported that it had been gifted to the National Trust the previous year.

It has been, and still is being, extensively excavated with a long history of digs, the first in earnest being carried out by one Mr John Clayton. Mr Clayton, whose family had lived at Chesters, had purchased much of the land adjacent to the wall to ensure that there could be a reversal to the salvaging of stone. He is seen as being a key figure in the saving of the wall for future generations. The wall to the west of Housesteads is known as Clayton's wall following his restorations, which including turfing it to facilitate walking along it.

After the transfer of ownership in 1930, there was a resurgence of excavations with particular efforts concentrated on the civilian habitats that had grown up around the fort itself. This civil community, known as the vicus, provided for one especially gruesome find when the bodies of a man and woman were found under the floor of a building that is now known as the 'murder house'. The location of the bodies was suspicious in itself because the Romans had designated burial areas but made even more intriguing by the fact that the male still had a knife blade between his ribs!

In G. Bernard Wood's book Secret Britain, he refers to this find being made in 1932, which was a year when a major dig was undertaken. While the accuracy of his account cannot be corroborated, it is interesting that by the time of Collingwood's ninth edition in 1937, his comprehensive description of Housesteads makes no reference to this extraordinary find which, all these years later, is probably the single most fascinating aspect of the fort for most schoolboys.

Housesteads (or whichever name you choose to use) is an illuminating part of Roman life (and death) hereabouts but we must press on westwards through probably the most dramatic switchback territory of the wall as it rides the waves of the escarpment. The views are spectacular to both the east and the west and the sheer magnificence of the Roman engineering achievement has to be seen to be believed.

We have once again joined the Pennine Way, for its way and ours share the same route from Turret 37A through to our leaving the wall at the early part of tomorrow's walk (other than for our diversion for an overnight break at Haltwhistle). We encounter another association with more recent history as we proceed down a steep slope at the west end of Crag Lough – the dip with the lone sycamore tree is famous as the tree used in the 1991 film Robin Hood: Prince of Thieves and is now known as Sycamore Gap.

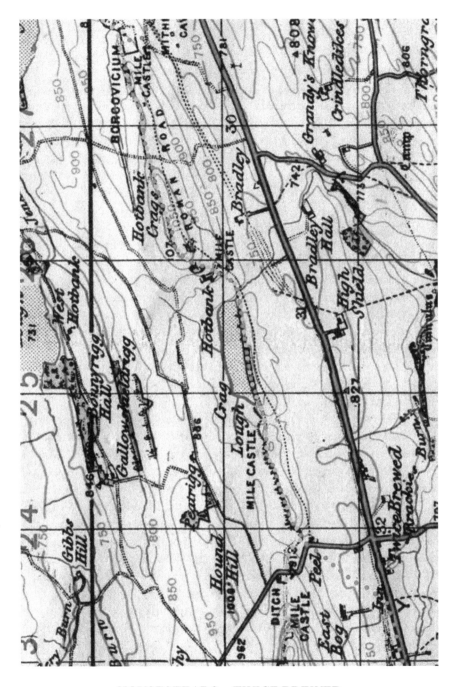

HOUSESTEADS – TWICE BREWED

DAY NO. 6/MAP NO.6 TWICE BREWED – HALTWHISTLE

This most spectacular of days is drawing to a close and I defy anyone to have a day more enveloped in history than on this one. For the most part we have shared a history from nigh on 1,800 years ago but more recent history will still give a tad of interest as we near day's end.

It is a mystery why AW left the wall where he did when he proceeded to leave it west of Milecastle 39 near Peel and toward the strangely named hamlet of Twice Brewed. Ours, on the other hand, takes all opportunity to follow the wall and it seems unlikely that a detour to the Twice Brewed Inn will be possible unless you choose to overnight there rather than at Haltwhistle.

The origin of the inn's name is to be found in stories that relate back to the time of the building of the Military Road around 1750. It is said that the beer, being weak, was not to the navvies' liking and so it was brewed again, and henceforth referred to by its modern name. Although this may seem like a rather fanciful tale is it just pure coincidence that in a Haltwhistle graveyard there is a gravestone to one William Porthouse, born in 1752, with the inscription reading that he was from Twice Brewed Ale?

Further investigation in the Durham Probate Records includes a reference to a William Porthouse being the innkeeper at the Twice Brewed Inn. So perhaps there is truth in the tale. There is further intrigue in local names at the adjacent Once Brewed, to which no reference is made on the AW map. The reason for this seems to again relate to a historical event, this time from the twentieth century.

The YHA was growing rapidly in the years prior to the Second World War, with the local hostel being opened in 1934 by the ardent teetotaler Lady Trevelyan. In her speech at the opening she said there would be 'no alcohol served on these premises, and I hope the tea and coffee will be brewed only once'. Once Brewed, therefore, derives from around this time, which would explain why it does not appear on the old map.

We continue along the Hadrian's Wall trail as far as Milecastle 42 beyond Cawfield Crags, where a path leads south to a minor road that we follow for a short distance to the B6318. We then cross to follow Shield Hill down to Haltwhistle and care is needed on this road as it twists and turns on its descent to the town that did not meet with AW's blessing.

AW considered Haltwhistle to be the antithesis of Hexham; one being gay and charming and the other dejected and sullen. He had stayed at the Grey Bull Inn, as did I when I first visited in 1998. It has since closed but is now a bed and breakfast that is held in high regard by its visitors. It is likely that AW's observations back in 1938 were a fair judgement of a town going through major changes.

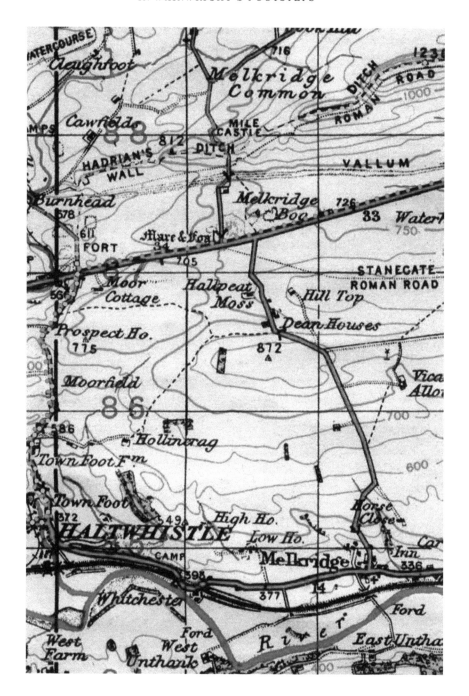

TWICE BREWED – HALTWHISTLE

DAY NO. 7

HALTWHISTLE TO ALSTON

DAY NO. 7

HALTWHISTLE TO ALSTON

Whatever misfortune has befallen Haltwhistle in more recent years, for the first part of today's walk we will be steeped in the town's history as we head north up Haltwhistle Burn. Long before the coming of the railway the burn was at the centre of local industry.

Reaching the wall again, we will encounter the destruction at Walltown, where quarrying was allowed to eat into the route of the wall and perhaps it was this that began to darken AW's mood as he accepted that his escapade was coming to an end.

Heading south toward South Tynedale valley, we can savour the walk along the track bed of the old railway and witness the fascinating remains of the old prisoner of war camp at Featherstone Castle.

We have joined the Pennine Way on most of our days and today we will visit it again, associating with the Romans again as we follow an old Roman road in South Tynedale.

Leg	From:	To:
7 – 1	Haltwhistle	Walltown
7 – 2	Walltown	Blenkinsopp Common
7 – 3	Blenkinsopp Common	Lambley
7 – 4	Lambley	Knarsdale
7 – 5	Knarsdale	Kirkside
7 – 6	Kirkside	Alston

Today's walk is approximately 19 miles, with no navigation problems and mainly straightforward walking along well-established tracks. At the end of the day we will arrive at what is reputedly England's highest market town, Alston, where once again we will find ourselves among the ancient lead miners of long ago.

Two maps are needed for the day from the Ordnance Survey 'Outdoor Leisure' series:

OL43   Hadrian's Wall (Hexham and Haltwhistle

OL31   North Pennines (Teesdale and Weardale)

We can enjoy most of the day's walk on paths and quiet tracks, except over Blenkinsopp Common where care needs to be taken following the road with its absence of pavements.

DAY NO. 7/MAP NO.1 HALTWHISTLE – WALLTOWN

It is abundantly clear that Haltwhistle has suffered some injustices over the years and it is evident that among the town's previous eras of decline one such episode was during the 1930s, which AW would have witnessed for himself on his encounter. The town's development was based upon textile manufacture and agriculture, and it expanded very rapidly after its transport links were vastly improved by the opening of the railway in 1838. At about the same time, the collieries opened on the Haltwhistle Burn and at Plenmeller. In 1852 the Alston branch was opened, which saw the lead-mining output coming through Haltwhistle and by the end of the decade it had become a prosperous mining town. The railway also provided for growth in the agricultural and textile sectors and the supply of lead even led to paint manufacture in the town.

The coal and lead industries within the region began to wane in the early years of the twentieth century and the South Tyne Colliery closed in 1931. This, allied to the impact of the depression, sounded the death knell for the town that AW had sensed. Sixty years later in 1998, I discovered at the Grey Bull that a self-effacing humour existed amongst the customers about the greyness of the town. There were boarded-up shops and a general feeling of a town that had seen happier days. It seemed that just about everything that had once been open was now firmly closed.

Haltwhistle now fares better, with something of a buzz about the place; it also has a new hospital and community centre. It is the nearest town of any size to the central section of the Roman Wall and perhaps this has boosted the tourist trade. Perhaps those same visitors will also savour soaking up Haltwhistle's rich industrial heritage. How strange that the industries that were central to the death of the town might now bring new life.

Nowhere can that heritage be better witnessed than following the path to Haltwhistle Burn and then following its course north. Our route follows Willia Road along the west bank of the burn and then, at Broomshaw Hill Farm, we follow the path, part of which was the track bed of the narrow-gauge railway, which ran the length of the burn from Cawfields Quarry down into Haltwhistle. The course of the track can be seen on the old map but it is now long gone, having become redundant, coincidentally, in 1938.

We cross the Military Road and make our way to Great Chesters Fort, turning west along the line of the wall, which is more of a grassy mound here. We have been spoiled by our encounters of yesterday but the wall's route will test your stamina as you ascend and descend the Nicks of Thirlwall.

These nicks have been formed as part of the whin sill and were originally nine separate outcrops – don't try accounting for all nine because, sadly, their separation has been disfigured by earlier quarrying of the bedrock on which the wall sits.

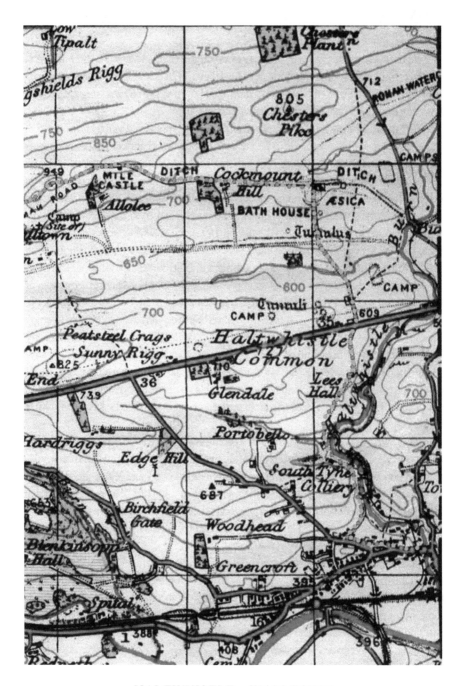

HALTWHISTLE – WALLTOWN

DAY NO. 7/MAP NO.2 WALLTOWN – BLENKINSOPP COMMON

We must savour this last part of our walk along the wall, for after our short acquaintance we will very soon be leaving it. There have been some great highpoints both emotionally and topographically and we must contrast these with a most singular, distinct low point as we approach the remnants of Walltown Quarry.

After passing the Nicks of Thirlwall we arrive at a well preserved turret, known as 45A. Just a few yards to the west of the turret the land simply disappears from under our feet as we stare into the abyss of the quarry.

Walltown Quarry began its destruction of the wall in 1877 with the turret 45B being destroyed in 1883, swallowed up as the quarrying headed eastwards along the line of the escarpment in the search for profit. John Clayton must have been distressed to witness this wanton destruction in his later years (he died in 1892); the quarrying works continued unabated until closure in 1977. Prior to the closure of the quarry, some years of falling output in the 1960s had helped to swell the unemployment of Haltwhistle.

So, although the quarry is in itself an impressive sight, it is also yet another example of the power that man has over his landscape, and the havoc that he is capable of wreaking. However, we must satisfy ourselves that we have been very fortunate to be able to enjoy what is without doubt the most dramatic section of the wall. The majesty of the topography in the central section from Limestone Bank all the way to Walltown is not equalled anywhere else along the wall. In fact, the magnificence of the wall that we have seen exists only as a small proportion; the wall is largely invisible on the surface over the vast majority of its length. Throughout its course, over 90 per cent of the wall is recorded as not visible on the surface.

Finally we must leave the wall, and in so doing we also leave the Pennine Way for the timebeing; we will join it again for a short while further south on today's walk. At this point AW's mood began to darken and he wrote 'my enthusiasm I had left at the Wall'. He viewed the journey south as a spiritless affair. His state of mind had been badly affected by the disastrous results of his photographic efforts when he had collected his ruined prints from the Haltwhislte chemist. He stated that this had ruined his intention to write a book with first class illustrations.

Much of AW's route on his trek south from the Wall seems to have been arrived at by finding the most direct route and we begin to see this from the time that he left the inn at Greenhead. He followed hard road surfaces for nearly all the way to Alston, a distance of some 14 miles. Our way and his will diverge for much of the remainder of this day and we will find much of interest in the history of the South Tyne valley, albeit very much more recent than we experienced yesterday.

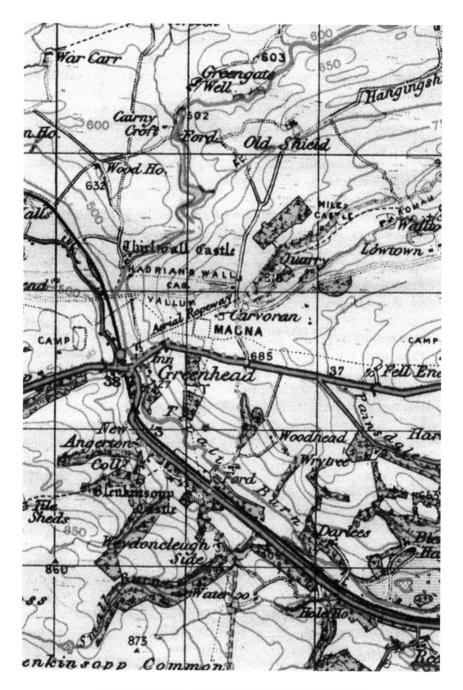

WALLTOWN – BLENKINSOPP COMMON

DAY NO. 7/MAP NO.3 BLENKINSOPP COMMON – LAMBLEY

In leaving the wall AW had walked to Greenhead but our route will turn south on the minor road, crossing the Military Road to find the path toward College Farm and on to the A69 Carlisle–Newcastle road. AW had walked from Greenhead along the main road toward Haltwhistle before turning off south, signposted Blenkinsopp Castle Inn.

Immediately after turning south the inn is reached, which is built from the extended ruins of Blenkinsopp Castle. The castle, a former tower house, had been developed into a hotel when AW passed by but was severely damaged by fire in 1954. After partial demolition in the 1960s, it was redeveloped and extended into the hotel that is here now.

The road south from the inn leads us to a major decision. AW referred to the 'Maiden Way', a Roman road heading south from Greenhead, but finding its actual route is a sufficiently difficult task to render trying to follow it foolhardy. He chose to follow the road over Blenkinsopp Common and toward the River South Tyne at Featherstone Bridge.

At the bridge, we now have the option to cross and follow the path to join the course of the old railway linking Haltwhistle and Alston. The South Tyne Trail would, if opted for, provide a route all the way to day's end that was not an option for AW, as the railway was in operation until as late as 1976.

Having no desire to slavishly suffer AW's route, I had chosen to follow riverside paths along the west bank of the river with the imposing Featherstone Castle on the opposite bank. The old map shows delightful green parkland surrounding the castle but on the modern map there is reference to a disused camp site. This is not a tent-based campsite as the evidence of buildings bears testament to. The shattered remnants are all that remains of a Second World War camp that was originally built in 1944 to house American forces prior to the D-Day invasion.

After the GIs had departed, the camp was brought back into use as a PoW camp, initially for Italians and latterly for 'Black Nazis' captured following the D-Day invasion. These were mainly officers of the German military who were the most fervent followers of Hitler's vision, and it was considered that they required serious denazification before being repatriated.

The camp was one the largest in the UK and the only one to house captured officers, Wehrmacht and SS. In all, over 7,000 officers were held here before the last man was returned to Germany in 1948, some three years after the end of the war. A memorial has been placed at the camp to Captain Herbert Sulzbach OBE, who dedicated himself to making this camp a seedbed of British–German reconciliation. He held the key post of Interpreter Officer from December 1945 until the camp closed in 1948.

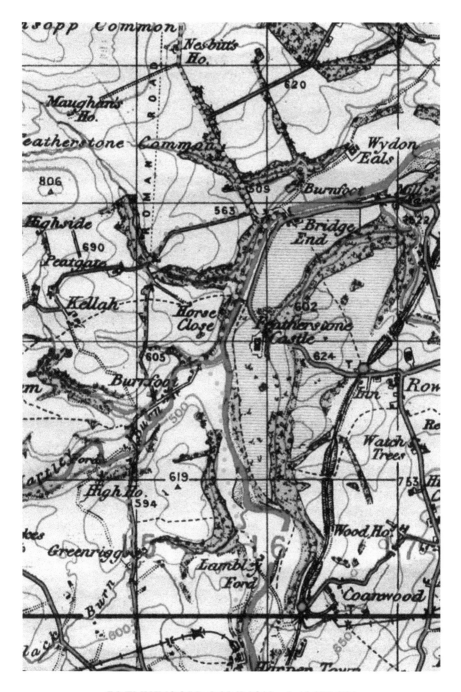

BLENKINSOPP COMMON – LAMBLEY

DAY NO. 7/MAP NO.4 LAMBLEY – KNARSDALE

Our riverside path leaves the bank of the river opposite the southern end of the old PoW camp and we arrive at the 'new road' at Lambley Farm. We have to then follow the road for a short while into the hamlet of Lambley. I am torn as to deciding the best route, for if we had followed the east side of the river we would have the pleasure in crossing the River South Tyne via the majestic Lambley viaduct. However, the west side allows us the chance to rejoin the Pennine Way and enjoy a couple of miles following the 'Maiden Way'.

The 'new road' referred to is the road that does not show on AW's map because at the time it did not exist, only having been built in 1976, and it played an integral part in the final demise of the railway. The South Tyne Railway had been built to serve the industry of the lead mines of the Alston and Nenthead areas and was opened in 1852. It also provided a rail link to the Lambley Colliery and the associated mineral line can be seen on the old map (and its course can still be made out on satellite mapping).

On the map contemporary with AW's trek, the hamlet is noted as Harper Town but the station serving the local community took its name from the farm some way to the north, Lambley. In the intervening years, the station name was included by the OS as the name of the community. Quite contrarily, one of the farms within the settlement is 'Harper Town Farm', so the hamlet has seen confusion over names down the years.

Even as the railway opened, the end of the line was nearing for the lead-mining industry in the area. The London Lead Company, who had taken over the lead extraction in the mid-eighteenth century, ceased activity in 1882 and left a major commercial aspect of the railway redundant. The coal mining at Lambley ceased in 1958 and sounded the final toll for the railway's commercial future.

The passenger traffic was accordingly affected by these reductions to commercial carrying and slowly the stations became unmanned to save money. This decline of the railway had been evident prior to the Beeching Report of 1963 but its stay of execution was secured as the railway was the only reliable means of bad weather transport. This proved so in 1963, when the valley was impassable for weeks by road but the railway stayed open. The valley had only limited road transport communications so the railway provided the only reliable means of access throughout the valley. The 'new road' of 1976 was provided to give improved road links and its building allowed the line to be closed.

Having rejoined the Pennine Way (via the 'Maiden Way'), we follow it south to Knarsdale, to the buildings that are noted on AWs map as Burnstones Inn. The inn used to have an informal 'halt' on the railway, with passengers clambering up or down the embankment to alight the trains which would, apparently, stop on a demand basis. We will do the same at this point to join the South Tyne Trail.

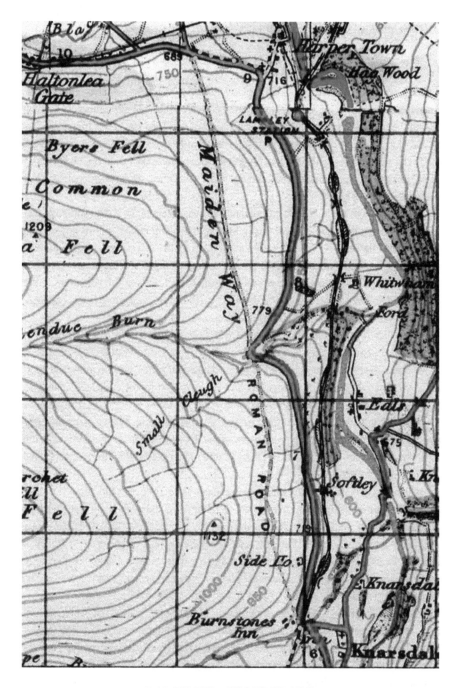

LAMBLEY – KNARSDALE

DAY NO. 7/MAP NO.5 KNARSDALE – KIRKSIDE

If you have a need for refreshment, Knarsdale has an inn, but bear in mind that it has limited opening hours. We will find no places to stop beyond the Kirkstyle Inn until we reach our destination at Alston. Having joined the South Tyne Trail, we turn south, heading toward the unusual sounding hamlet of Slaggyford. It was here that AW's mood lifted as he found the place to be very much more pleasant than its name suggests and he found food. The village still has much to commend it, but finding food would not be one of its strong points, nor would making any enquiry at the post office, for it has gone the way of many others before it.

Passing the quaint timber station building, it is easy to imagine a stopping-point that would have been the pride of the stationmaster, with hanging baskets full of flowers and neatly tended flowerbeds. When I passed this way in 1998, such reminiscence required a greater imagination for the overgrown remains of the platform and the decaying timber station building looked very much worse for wear. Now, however, the volunteers of the South Tyne Railway are working towards reopening the line to Slaggyford and in readiness the station-building has been brought back to its former glory.

The valley of the South Tyne is littered with coal seams that, due to the topography, were able to be mined using adits rather than vertical shafts. Evidence of this can be seen as we continue south along the track bed to the next halt along what was the railway at Lintley. AW's map shows an aerial ropeway and this was used by the Barhaugh colliery to bring coal from the mine on the hillside down to the valley floor.

Although the mine was closed for commercial mining in 1932, it has, along with many others in the area, had periods of productivity since. It was opened as a small venture in the 1990s by a group of four partners but the foot and mouth outbreak in 2001 was the final death knell for the hill collieries of the South Tyne.

Although we could continue to follow the South Tyne Trail, it would be good to visit the church on the eastern bank of the river, so Lintley to Kirkhaugh is our last stretch of delightful trackside walking. On reaching the station at Kirkhaugh we leave the South Tyne Trail and follow a track toward the river, heading for the ford that was noted on AW's map. Fear not, for as AW found, we do not need to ford the water; indeed it would be foolhardy in the extreme to attempt to ford the river and the sturdy Kirkhaugh footbridge will see us across with dry feet.

As we reach the bridge, we join another long distance trail, Isaac's Tea Trail. The trail takes its name from a lead miner, Isaac Holden who, when illness struck and recession hit lead mining, became an itinerant tea seller plying his trade from Alston over the moors to Allendale. He went on to become a prolific fundraiser for good causes and a memorial can be found in Allendale at the start of the 36-mile circular route.

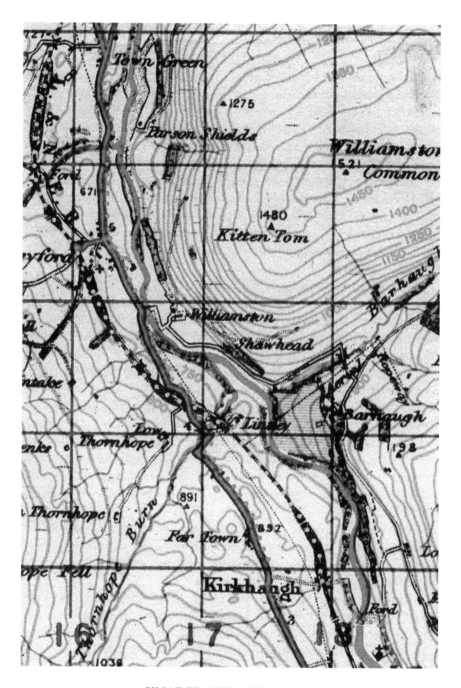

KNARSDALE – KIRKSIDE

DAY NO. 7/MAP NO.6 KIRKSIDE – ALSTON

Following Isaac's Tea Trail, we join the narrow byway leading toward Kirkside Woods and we very soon encounter the very individual church serving Kirkhaugh. The Holy Paraclete Parish Church is the only one in England with such a dedication and is presumably the reason for the ford for the parishioners. How they were to reach the church without wet feet is unclear! It was built on a previously sacred site and it may be that the footbridge across the river dates from this time to try to keep congregation numbers up.

The church was built in 1849 having been designed by its rector, one Octavius James, with its unusual spire influenced by his earlier travels in the Black Forest. The spire has received widely mixed reviews, with AW himself describing it as 'thin and weedy', musing that the designer must have been horrified when the builder showed him the finished job. Of course, we now know that Rector James knew what to expect for his very individual church.

We follow Isaac's Tea Trail as far as Randalholm Bridge, where the trail heads off up the Ayle Burn valley and we keep to the unclassified road over the bridge. Since we first walked into Blanchland, we have had Northumberland under our feet but now, having crossed to Randalholme, we have moved into a new county, Cumbria, in which we will remain until beyond Deepdale on our final day's walk.

If you look beyond the sprawling twentieth-century additions at Randalholm, there is evidence of both a pele tower and a bastle, with a very long history dating back to 1370 with many further additions (before the rather less attractive single-storey agricultural buildings).

Our route and AW's coincide for the last stretch into Alston itself, and the narrow lane leads through a delightful tree-lined avenue arriving at Alston by the old railway station. The station is now a hive of activity as the terminus of the narrow-gauge South Tynedale Railway with the old goods shed now housing the Hub Museum, a fascinating insight into local life and history.

AW arrived at Alston on the day of the Alston Show, the last one held prior to the outbreak of the Second World War, and as he did so Alston was alive with partygoers; many of them extended the day's celebrations into the early hours at what was known as the Alston hoppings, followed by the Town Hall dance.

His visit was remembered by one ex-resident of the town, Muriel Thompson, who, as a young girl in 1938 recalled vividly the excitement that was felt throughout the town on show day. The show parade, accompanied by the brass band, would have made its way down from Town Head to the showground on the Tyne Willows Field. AW was not in much of a mood for such revelry, admitting that he was 'a wee bit depressed'.

KIRKSIDE – ALSTON

DAY NO. 8

ALSTON TO SLAKE'S FARM/KNOCK

DAY NO. 8

ALSTON TO SLAKE'S FARM/KNOCK

Today is the day when our way and AW's have the most significant of divergences. He chose, wisely, to give up on Cross Fell and follow the Hartside Moor road, which involves mile after mile of interminable roadside walking drudgery. The Pennine Way was not in existence back then and is well marked on the ground, so hopefully we will not have to follow him, for I feel sure he wouldn't want us to.

The vast majority of Day 8 follows the Pennine Way and we could choose to also use it to descend into the Eden valley if preferred.

The end of Day 8's walking reflects what I had chosen to do but it may be that the walk can be extended to reach a greater degree of civilisation. I had decided (and was pleased I did) that after a day over Cross Fell I might be glad of a slightly shorter mileage. Cross Fell itself represents the only threat to progress and I can only warn against complacency for the weather can change very quickly. Take care and your Pennine journey won't end as a statistic!

The day is divided into six sections with reference to Knock Pike only being to identify the general area; I am not proposing to ascend the pike at the end of such a day.

Leg	From:	To:
8 – 1	Alston	Dryburn Bridge
8 – 2	Dryburn Bridge	Pikeman Hill
8 – 3	Pikeman Hill	Skirwith Fell
8 – 4	Skirwith Fell	Great Dunn Fell
8 – 5	Great Dunn Fell	Knock Pike
8 – 6	Knock Pike	Slake's Farm/Knock

Today's walk again is approximately 20 miles and although there are few navigation difficulties, care should be exercised in traversing Cross Fell, especially if inclement weather is forecast. The majority of the day's walking follows the Pennine Way, so is well waymarked. The day's walk destination, noted as Slake's Farm/Knock, is not a mark of indecision but simply reflects the general location of where I had stayed in 1998. It transpires that bed and breakfast is no longer available at the farm and Knock has been identified as a neighbouring alternative, although accommodation here is very limited, hence the suggestion to marginally lengthen the day's walk to find greater choice of an overnight stop.

There exists little opportunity for refreshment so a packed lunch is highly recommended. Beyond Garrigill there is nothing other than an upland eerie landscape pitted with the remnants of a time when these hills were very much more populated in the days of active lead mining.

Two maps are required for the day's walk from the Ordnance Survey 'Outdoor Leisure' series:

OL31   North Pennines (Teesdale and Weardale)

OL19   Howgill Fells & Upper Eden Valley

Today is a hard walk and it would be best to allow 9 hours and slightly longer if alternative accommodation were to be sought at Long Marton.

slaggyford station

AW recalled very fondly his stay in Alston, spent in the company of the Richardson family. Although he had been exhausted and a little depressed when he arrived, he had still made his way up the steep main street to Townhead looking for accommodation.

Mr Richardson had been heavily involved with show day as he was secretary of the poultry section and AW's evening had been filled with the comings and goings of the locals seemingly calling to regale newsworthy gossip of who was doing what at the hoppings. The hoppings was a north country term for a general beano with fair and stalls and always a dance, no doubt hence the name. Perhaps we too can recall going the hop long before hanging out at the disco.

Richardson was by no means an uncommon surname in Alston which has resulted in something of an inconclusive search for details of AW's host. A visit to The Hub museum in the old engine shed reveals a picture of the show committee from 1945 where two of the members, Laurie and Joseph, both had the surname Richardson.

It may be though that the search is at an end, for Muriel Thompson's recollections include the fact that the Townhead Richardson of poultry connection was one Ridley Richardson of Crossfell View. This would generally correspond to AW's description of the house for the Crossfell View properties still stand as a row of small terraced houses in Townhead.

Much of today's walk follows the route of the Pennine Way and we start the day at Townfoot, turning left just before the bridge over the river. AW had decided to follow the Penrith road toward Leadgate. Even though a path was shown on his map to the east of the river, it seems likely that, as he was proposing to reach Appleby, he had a need for speed rather than follow an unknown path.

At the start of the day, AW had still been intending to summit Cross Fell, but as both the weather and his mood worsened he decided at Leadgate to proceed via the Hartside road and give up on his original route. He consoled himself afterwards that it was the only reasonable course and records from that time suggest that had he not taken the 'cowardly' option he may not have been around to produce his Pictorial Guides!

The weather in the north-west on that October day back in 1938 was under the influence of an intense Atlantic depression, which resulted in severe gales and prolonged rainfall. Not too far away at Watendlath in his beloved Lakes 475 mm of rain fell in ten days from 2 October. AW passed this way on 2 October 1938 so it is easy to see how the remaining days of his trek were dogged with horrendous weather.

That path shown on AW's map up above the eastern bank of the river is now the Pennine Way and we follow it until we cross via the footbridge near Dryburn Farm.

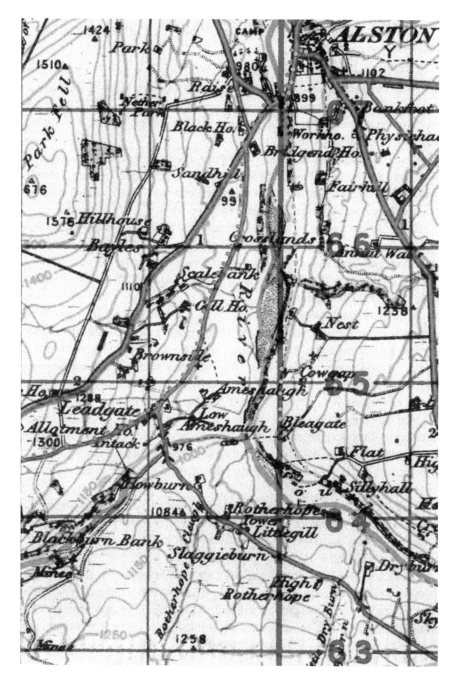

ALSTON – DRYBURN BRIDGE

DAY NO. 8/MAP NO.2 DRYBURN BRIDGE – PIKEMAN HILL

As we head up the valley on the second section of the day's walk for the first time we see no sign of the route taken by AW on our route map. He was trudging up the long road ascent toward Hartside Cross having decided against attempting Cross Fell. Bearing in mind that for centuries earlier the hill was known as Fiend's Fell, his choice on that day back in 1938 was perhaps wise.

Armed with map, compass, GPS, good clothing, a belief in oneself and a propensity to avoid panic the way up and over the fell should not present too much difficulty. There is now a well waymarked route and even some rather rudimentary accommodation to be had, should we really need it. We will hear more of that later.

Back in the valley of the South Tyne, once across the footbridge over the river the Pennine Way finds its way via a riverside path to Garrigill, which we enter along the quiet road at Gatefoot. The village was originally known as Garrigill Gate but the use of the suffix has been lost with the use of Gatefoot for the lower end and Gatehead for the upper end perhaps being a reminder of the previous, longer name.

We are very much back in lead-mining country and the village has its origins in hill mining. Reference to parish records reveals just how many of the births and deaths related to a populous that was steeped in lead mining. Back in the day the village boasted two inns, the George and Dragon and the Old Fox. The Old Fox, adjacent to the church, has long since closed and the remaining inn has suffered spells of closure in recent years. It is therefore perhaps best that we don't assume we will be availed of refreshment.

Even though the village lies on both the Pennine Way and the Coast to Coast cycle route it struggles to keep one inn busy and the population, which once counted 1,000, is nowadays approximately 200. The demise of the lead mines began the steady depopulation of the area as a whole and the ascent of Cross Fell will bear witness to the extent of the local lead industry.

We leave Garrigill at Gatehead via a quiet byway that soon develops into an unmade track. It is well way marked for we are still following the route of the Pennine Way. It is a 7-mile walk to reach the summit of Cross Fell, the vast majority being on a clear track with no navigation difficulties.

The track is the old lead miners' route and it passes an eerie collection of mining detritus to either side. I have passed this way in a severe drizzling mist and in such conditions it becomes very easy to mistake perfectly innocent objects for ghoulish apparitions. In AW's Pennine Way Companion, he advises that it is best to keep to the track for the path that shows 'cutting the corner' is unclear on the ground.

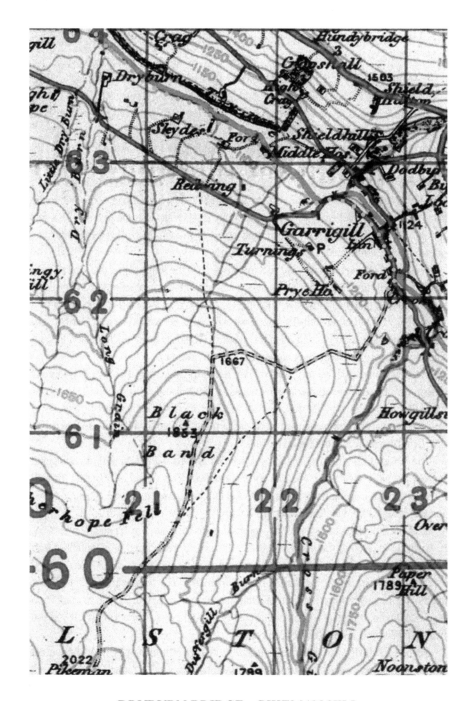

DRYBURN BRIDGE – PIKEMAN HILL

DAY NO. 8/MAP NO.3 PIKEMAN HILL – SKIRWITH FELL

If we are lucky with the weather, the views will be opening up as we gain height on the steady ascent. The track is sound underfoot and I suggest making sure we stick to its course, for this whole area is pitted with shakeholes. To go astray in these unforgiving environs might be the last time that a person errs.

Passing just to the west of Pikeman Hill, the path follows south toward Long Man Hill with relics of previous mining activity to both sides of the track. The path remains clear and navigation would only create difficulties if the track were to be left. This is not a walk I would relish after a fresh deep snowfall. A short way after the path changes direction to the south-west, just beyond Black Gut, there is a more direct route to reach Cross Fell's summit, but in AW's Pennine Way account he warns of needing to beware of open shafts. Adhering to the main route is both easier and safer.

Were it to be that on our way we become ensnared in the foul weather that Cross Fell is very capable of throwing at any who enter its lair, then there is at least some very basic accommodation that might just save your life. On the old map there is a reference to a lead mine to the west of Fallow Hill. This mine was known as Screeds Mine and, being a very long way from any form of civilisation, the workers would stay near the mine in a lodging house (Flushimere House in Teesdale served a similar purpose).

In the late nineteenth century, lead mining began to wane as cheaper ore from abroad undermined the market and the lodging house fell into disuse and disrepair. It lay abandoned for many years until hill walking became a more popular pastime and the benefits of such remote places were recognised as having a use as refuge for hill walkers that might have found themselves in trouble on the fells.

The Mountain Bothies Association was formed in 1965 with the aim of providing and maintaining basic shelters for hill walkers and climbers. This would be achieved through the restoration of existing buildings, such as the lodging house on Cross Fell, and permission was received from the landowner in 1969 to carry out the required work.

At about the same time as AW was completing his Pennine Way Companion in 1968, in which he referred to the hut as a 'ruined cottage', he recognised its possibility as an emergency bivouac. Unbeknown to AW, in April 1968 a climber had died in the Alps and his climbing colleagues were seeking a suitable memorial. The climber was John Gregory, and the memorial was the restoration of what became known as Greg's Hut, as marked on the modern map. It is great work that this charity does so please make sure that if you use their hospitality you respect the Bothy Code.

Beyond the bothy, the path climbs a few more metres to the watershed where a tall cairn, the Yad Stone, marks the point at which we must turn south for the final ascent.

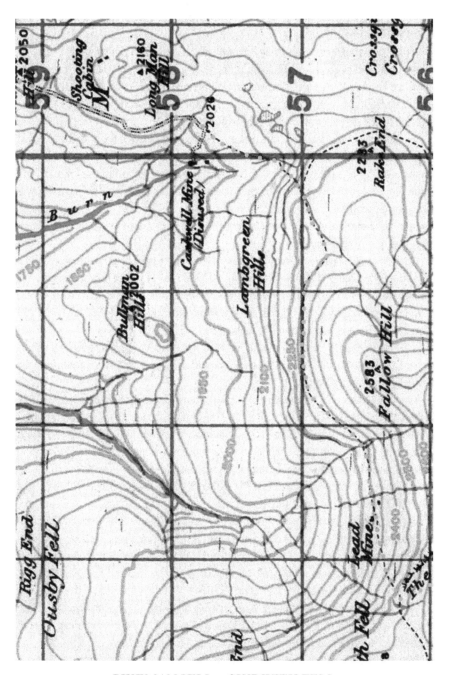

PIKEMAN HILL – SKIRWITH FELL

DAY NO. 8/MAP NO.4 SKIRWITH FELL – GREAT DUNN FELL

The final part of the ascent to the plateau summit of Cross Fell leads through a boulder-strewn wasteland where the path is indistinct and bearings can be easily lost in poor visibility. Once beyond the boulders, we can stroll amongst the collection of various summit paraphernalia, the largest of which is the cross-wall shelter where some respite can be sought from the gale that will doubtless be blowing.

In AW's first Pictorial Guide, the Eastern Fells, he dedicates the volume to the men of the Ordnance Survey for providing him not only with help on the fells but also for entertainment by the fireside. It is clear that he found most pleasure in his love of maps and indeed on this eighth day, which had ended prematurely at Gamblesby, he spent the evening poring over his maps planning his remaining days. He talked of being happy to spend hours in close study of a map and its contours and features; a map would tell him a story more than any text book could do.

On the plateau summit of Cross Fell, we arrive at the triangulation point denoted on the modern map by means of a small blue triangle. This, and all other trig points, dates back to the nationwide retriangulation survey that was commenced in 1936. It was undertaken to provide a replacement to the original measurements that had been carried out some 150 years earlier. So, had AW reached the top of Cross Fell in 1938, he might have wondered as to the use of the new piece of summit furniture. Many such trig points were maintained by the OS until the mid-1980s when new electronic and GPS-based systems rendered the triangulation method obsolete.

On the old map, all summits are shown with a small black solid triangle and it was only in the later OS map series that the modern symbol began to be used. AW's maps are likely to have been of the 'Popular Edition' range because the 'Fifth Edition', which had been under preparation during the 1930s, had only extended as far north as Oxford before being curtailed with the outbreak of the Second World War, when the 'War Revision' copies were then published, largely based on the earlier 'Popular Edition'. It follows then that AW's maps must have been of the earlier issue.

From the trig point our route is south-easterly to Tees Head at the watershed between east and west, into the col and up onto Little Dunn Fell. We then repeat the down and up to reach the summit of Great Dunn Fell; in the Pennine Way Companion AW had felt embittered about the summit's ruination at the hands of air traffic controllers and weather forecasters.

The path between the three tops is very clear, following the Pennine Way via stone flagging, and we leave the radar station with a choice of ways. Nevertheless, in poor weather and visibility be very careful not to go astray for this was the only place where, left to my own natural senses, without aid of map and compass, I would have turned north rather than south. Beware, you have been warned.

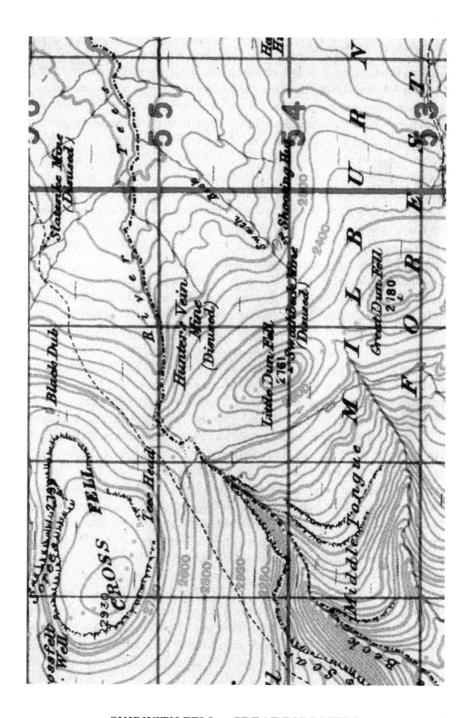

SKIRWITH FELL – GREAT DUNN FELL

DAY NO. 8/MAP NO.5 GREAT DUNN FELL – KNOCK PIKE

The summit gadgets on Great Dunn Fell perhaps appear less unsightly than back in the day when AW berated them. The single sphere and reduced number of masts are easier on the eye, although I suspect it is doubtful that AW would agree. Beyond the station we can, I would suggest, descend into the Eden valley directly by means of the station's access road. The service road, recently resurfaced, is the highest macadam road in the UK, and if the weather is as it was when I passed this way you will be very glad to have found it and equally happy to follow it to the safety of the lower lands.

In crossing the three fells, we have achieved the three highest points of our trek; in fact Cross Fell is England's highest hill outside the Lake District. It also has another claim in that it has a close association with the UK's only named wind. The Helm Wind is a meteorological phenomenon particular to this area and can be caused when the surface wind is from the north-east, usually in the spring and autumn months.

Although other regions in the UK exhibit similar weather patterns, it is only on the Cross Fell range where it has earned the accolade of being named. The wind blows across the Pennine massif and upon reaching the escarpment of the eastern side of the Eden valley it accelerates down into the valley below, with an especial ferocity around Milburn.

The wind, which can blow for days at a time, takes its name from the cloud formation that is generally associated with its occurrences; the summit of Cross Fell is likely to be enveloped in a cloud formation similar to a helmet. The locals talk of the 'Helm's up' and the wind will arrive with a roar and has been known to knock sheep off their feet.

There are also other stories of the wind presented in Bernard Wood's North Country Profile of 1961 in which he relates that some years prior (in 1935), bunches of hay had been seen flying over Windermere at an estimated altitude of 2,000 feet. This is, I suspect, apocryphal as the wind rarely blows beyond the Eden valley. The wind has been the subject of considerable interest in further understanding of its origin, with probably the greatest being that undertaken by Gordon Manley in the late 1930s. A hut was installed at the top of Great Dunn Fell in 1936 to which he paid periodic visits in the hope of 'measuring' a helm experience. It would have been amusing to see what AW might have made of Manley's hut before the more extensive station stirred his displeasure. Following the service road down the valley of Knock Ore Gill will clearly not present any navigation problems. The alternative would be to continue on the Pennine Way via Knock Fell and Green Fell, ultimately descending into the village of Knock. If the Pennine Way path is followed from the summit then very soon we arrive at a striking relic of previous mining activity. The Dunfell Hush, just to the left of the path, is a man-made valley formed by the release of water from a dam construction to flush away the soil and reveal the mineral veins for extraction.

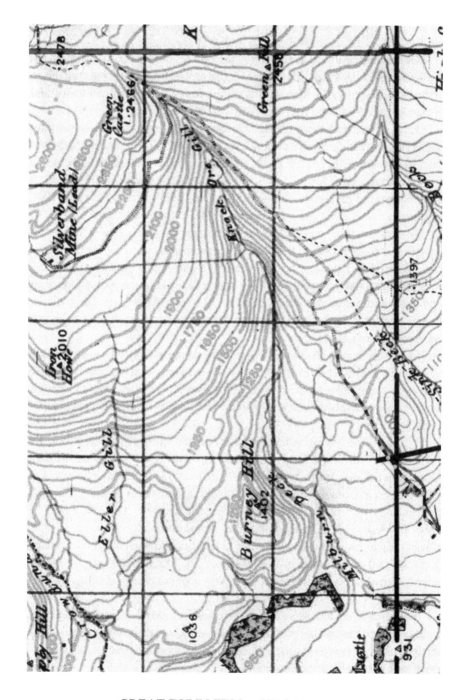

GREAT DUNN FELL – KNOCK PIKE

DAY NO. 8/MAP NO.6 KNOCK PIKE – SLAKE'S FARM/KNOCK

First, a point of clarification for it seems that there are two distinct destinations to this final section of the day's walk. My reason for including the farm is simply that I had chosen to stay there during my 1998 walk , but changes in circumstances mean that there is a need to consider an alternative end to this eighth day's excursion.

Our way continues a steady descent of the service road and as we descend we leave behind the last of our incursions into the relics of the lead mining heritage of the North Pennines. The geology of the area is such that lead ore is not found in the valley floors and the greatest concentration of mining activity is in the hills. The last mine of any size was at Silverband, owned by Laporte Chemicals from 1938, which mined byrates until 1963. Between the time of AW's visit and closure, over 200,000 tons were extracted.

The extracted ore was transported 3.5 miles down the fell side via an aerial ropeway for processing at Milburn Grange; from here it was transported on to mainline rail links at Long Marton. (The ropeway is not shown on AW's map because only after Laporte acquired the rights was the ropeway built – it takes time to incorporate such changes even with those good men of the Ordnance Survey.) The mine did see some late twentieth-century small-scale activity but this was not successful and it is now fully closed with little evidence of its previous status.

If, after your descent, you propose to stay at Knock, do not be fooled into thinking that an inn is still to be found; although AW's map showed a hostelry at the eastern end of the village your search will be in vain for it has gone the way of many others before it. Knock is largely a street-village and is not well furnished with facilities for overnight accommodation.

The major change in overnight lodging is that, in the course of research, it transpires that the Slake's Farm owners have retired and no longer provide bed and breakfast services. Allied to this is the fact that the inn I visited along the road to Milburn on my original trek in 1998, the Stag Inn, closed in 2006. Although bed and breakfast can be found at Lowgill Farm just to the north of Slake's Farm, this is extending our day's walk. In the light of the loss of the inns and lack of readily available accommodation, it may be that current route-planning might now extend Day 8 to reach Long Marton (or even off-route in Dufton) where there is a greater choice of accommodation. The Mason's Arms in Long Marton remains open at the time of writing and we can only hope that other local village history is not repeated.

The map directions include Slake's Farm because of the interest in seeing the remnants of the Laporte processing plant at Milburn Grange, which we will pass more closely at the early part of our ninth day. However, it is recognised that this will require a small degree of ingenuity in securing somewhere to overnight.

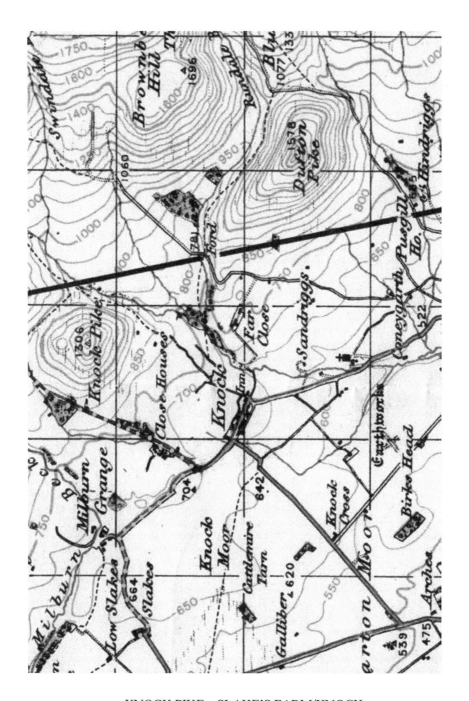

KNOCK PIKE – SLAKE'S FARM/KNOCK

DAY NO. 9

SLAKE'S FARM/KNOCK TO SOULBY

DAY NO. 9

SLAKE'S FARM/KNOCK TO SOULBY

Today is a gentle day that can be savoured. With some relief, we can look forward to our ninth day as altogether easier, with few hills to sap energy and less mileage. There will even be time to appreciate the delightful 'county town' of Appleby-in-Westmorland. The day's walk takes us south through the Eden valley with some options to investigate delightful Eden villages.

We come back together with AW at Long Marton but we part company again after Appleby as he was content to walk along the roadway to Soulby. Today comprises an afternoon of riverside walking following the River Eden as it meanders its way through the vale.

The day is split into five legs as follows:

Leg	From:	To:
9 – 1	Slake's Farm/Knock	Long Marton
9 – 2	Long Marton	Appleby
9 – 3	Appleby	Helm Beck
9 – 4	Helm Beck	Ploughlands
9 – 5	Ploughlands	Soulby

Day 9 is an easy day of 13 miles assuming a start at Knock. It is marginally less if starting out from Long Marton. There will be time to halt in Appleby-in-Westmorland and an opportunity to look around the town and find refreshment. Beyond the town there is little opportunity for food or drink stops and there is no welcoming inn at day's end.

The map required for the day is the 'Outdoor Leisure' series:

OL19   Howgill Fells and Upper Eden Valley

The amount of time to be allowed is governed by the choice of diversions. Allowing for a stop in Appleby, it would be best to allow 7 hours, adding an hour if a lunch break is taken in Sandford.

DAY NO. 9/MAP NO.1 SLAKE'S FARM/KNOCK – LONG MARTON

The details of the route for this first section will depend upon where the previous night has been spent. Assuming, however, a start from Slake's Farm, our route follows the minor road back to Milburn Grange. Still evident around the site are remnants of the buildings used in the processing of the barytes that arrived via the ropeway from Silverband Mine.

Following the access road to the right at the fork at the entrance to the self-contained cottages, a path leads through the various reminders of the Grange's earlier existence; foundation slabs of old huts and the stanchion bases of the earlier ropeway uprights. Our route crosses the fields heading south-east to Close House before following the road for a short distance, where we then take the path across the field toward Knock.

Entering Knock via an unmade track we then follow the road toward the inn marked on AW's map. The village inn is no more and there is little to delay us in passing through to find the path around the rear of the houses. The navigation to Long Marton is a little more complicated but our route follows field boundaries and farm tracks through Newlands Farm and then joins the Knock Cross road for a short way before following a path toward Birkshead Plantation.

Beyond Birks Head the path arrives at a track which we follow to join the Dufton to Long Marton road. Arriving in Long Marton, we finally rejoin AW after his joyless march through a selection of the Eden valley villages that he had described within one paragraph. He summed up his journey by writing that between Gamblesby and Appleby 'very little happened … that remains in memory'.

AW referred to Long Marton being alone among the villages in having a station. In 1938, Long Marton was the first call north of Appleby on the Settle to Carlisle railway. Built in 1875, it operated until May 1970 when it closed to passenger traffic. The platforms were ripped up soon after, with the locals being left with the sense that this was a cynical move by British Rail to ensure that any calls for the station's reopening would fail through lack of viability.

The station had seen a major commercial increase in traffic in 1941 when Laporte Chemicals extended the aerial ropeway from Milburn Grange to a purpose made hopper and sidings at the south end of the station to allow the loading of the barytes onto rail wagons.

At the junction we turn left, signposted to Appleby, and have to follow the road until the footpath immediately beyond the bridge over Trout Beck. After following the beck for 200 metres, a path to the left will take us to Church House and out onto the road, which we follow as far as the access track to Broad Lea.

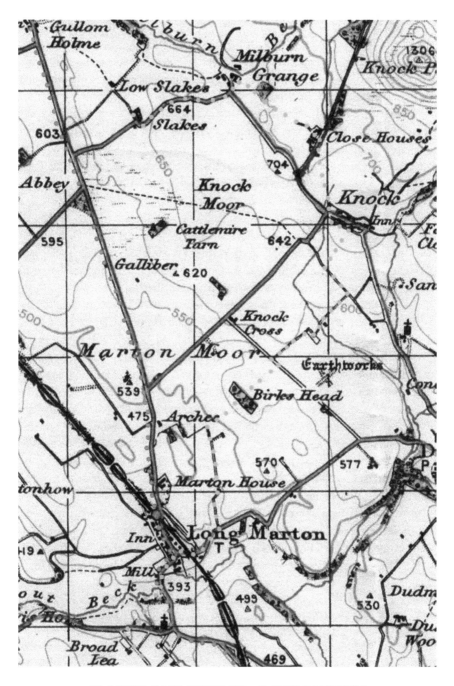

SLAKE'S FARM/KNOCK – LONG MARTON

DAY NO. 9/MAP NO.2 LONG MARTON – APPLEBY

The track extends beyond Broad Lea to reach Far Broom. Just prior to the farm, a path leads off to the right and follows the field boundary before joining the Roman road and heading south-east towards Appleby.

We follow the typically straight Roman road for approximately 1 mile to the very outskirts of the town. On AW's map, this track was shown as 'High Street' (although only the word 'street' can be seen on our route map) whereas on the modern map there is no reference other than to it being a Roman road. Those who are knowledgeable of the Lake District will know that High Street is one of the fells in the eastern Lakes that takes its name from the Roman road that follows its plateau summit.

The road over the summit runs between Ambleside and Brougham near Penrith and then follows eastwards into the Eden valley towards Brough. For the most part, the course of the road is largely lost as the A66 has been built over great sections of it. The longest section that survives is the bridleway that we follow to join the road where we turn right, finding ourselves having to walk on the footpath adjacent to the road into Appleby.

As we near the town, a nameplate gives the town its full name of Appleby-in-Westmorland. As a county, Westmorland was lost in the changes within the Local Government Act of 1972 when, from 1974, Cumberland and Westmorland (and parts of Yorkshire) lost their separate identities and became Cumbria. Appleby had been the county town of Westmorland and the local councilors were so aggrieved that they applied to formally rename it so that at least there would be an association with its heritage and history.

For many years, Appleby has been associated with a horse fair that is held in early June each year. The fair attracts many thousands of gypsies from far and wide who all use the occasion to trade horses and generally catch up with friends. It has also become a major tourist attraction with the town's population swelling by approximately 100,000 during the fair. It is held on Fair Hill, also known as Gallows Hill, which bears witness to its rather more gruesome previous use.

It would be very easy, especially for the car driver, to bypass the pleasures of Appleby for the main trunk road passes it by to the north-east. To miss such a place would be a shame for the main street, Boroughgate, has an old-world charm leading through its wide tree-lined avenue to the privately owned castle, which was once the home of Lady Anne Clifford. It was she who was largely responsible for its major reparation in the mid-seventeenth century after it suffered severe damage during the English Civil War.

Our route follows the road to the west of the castle with the tall perimeter wall preventing views of the castle beyond.

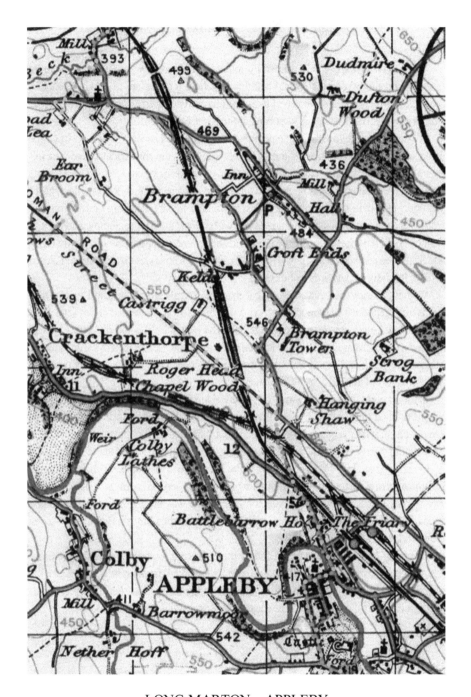

LONG MARTON – APPLEBY

DAY NO. 9/MAP NO.3 APPLEBY – HELM BECK

When AW left Appleby he did so by following the road toward Burrells, where he turned off on the byroad that would take him 'without a deviation, to Kirkby Stephen'. Once again, his choice of route is best to not be followed and from Appleby our way is far more preferable in following the west bank of the River Eden.

We continue to follow the castle perimeter wall to the left as we fork left down Castle Bank; where vehicle access ends, a path leads off towards the river bank. There then follows a delightful riverside walk that follows the river as far as where Jeremy Gill joins the main river. A steep path leads up through the wooded ravine and then follows the fields to pass under the Settle–Carlisle railway to then find a track into the village of Great Ormside.

AW's enthusiasm was fast-waning as he passed along the road to Soulby, and back in 1938 he could have turned left at the crossroads he referred to and found his way to Ormside Station, as marked on his map. The station, like many others, is no more having closed in 1952. It is now an outward-bound centre.

We have already seen evidence of great changes to rural communities and the Ormside area is no exception. The school shown on AW's map served the local children until 1968 when it closed, now serving as the village hall. The hospital just south of Great Ormside was opened in 1898 as the Ormside Hospital for Infectious Diseases to provide an isolation unit for diphtheria and smallpox. It later became a geriatric hospital for a short time, but now forms part of the Wild Rose Caravan Park.

In more recent times, Great Ormside gained an inn when, in 1987, the Dexters Inn was opened (named after a local trotting pony), having been formed from the conversion of Rectory Farm. It later became the Ormside Inn but sadly this too has gone, having closed in 2004 – it did at least once provide the winning tug-of-war team in a local fair at Warcop.

On arriving at Great Ormside, a walk to the left will lead to St James's church, built on a part-natural and part-man-made mound, which gives a good view of the ten-arched railway viaduct across the river. In 1823, the churchyard was the location of an important discovery in the form of an Anglo Saxon bowl. Known as the Ormside Bowl, it was given to the Yorkshire Museum in York.

Returning to the village, we then follow the quiet lane south-east toward Little Ormside, which consists of little more than Ormside Lodge and Terry's Farm, but does provide us with a sylvan saunter through this wonderfully quiet rural backwater. It is very much more appealing than contemplating a repeat of AW's most unsatisfactory road walk.

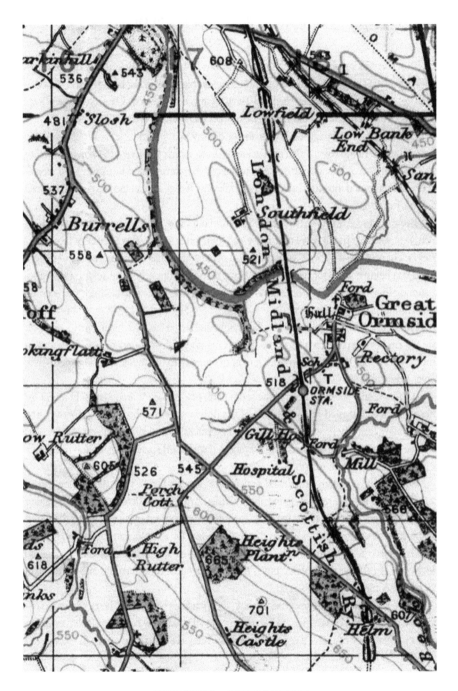

APPLEBY – HELM BECK

DAY NO. 9/MAP NO.4 HELM BECK – PLOUGHLANDS

The lane continues towards Little Ormside, crossing Helm Beck and rounding the corner to Ormside Lodge. Passing the magnificent example of the cedar tree, the lane's surface becomes more of a track than a road and Terry's Farm is the last outpost accessed via Ormside. We are now heading south-east, generally parallel with the river.

Proceeding towards Trickle Banks, the bridleway skirts Tricklebanks Wood and joins the south bank of the River Eden at Blacksyke, from which the access track is followed to Sandford Bridge. Although our route is to follow the narrow lane in front of the single-storey buildings and then turn left onto the bridleway, it may be that the hamlet of Sandford is worthy of a visit.

The Sandford Arms is somewhat remote from our route but if we have avoided rushing then it may be that it will serve as a fine place for a lunch break. There are very few hostelries on our route on this ninth day, so unless a packed lunch has been secured the inn might avoid you being hungry for the afternoon walk. It is approximately 1 mile extra walking so, assuming that a roaming internet access is possible, it would be wise to check the opening hours as the inn is not open every day.

From Sandford, we follow a broadly straight line while the river meanders to the north of Doll Brow. The path from Sandford follows the line of field boundaries before joining a track, which leads to a narrow byway and onto the road to the medieval bridge across the River Eden leading to Warcop.

Although our route is to keep to the south bank of the river, Warcop is worth a visit for those who are interested in the heritage of the railways for it is here that the rejuvenated Eden Valley Railway has its headquarters. The visitors' centre is very interesting, with an eclectic mix of railway paraphernalia. It is some distance off route so it's best to check that it is open before venturing forth.

Warcop mirrors many other rural settlements in that it has lost its village store and its post office and the sole remaining inn, the Chamley Arms, has suffered a chequered trading history in recent times. In times gone by, the village was served by five inns but the future of the sole survivor, once known as the Railway Inn for its association with the railway workers before being changed to its current name, is in doubt as developers have sought to develop it as self-catering holiday units. If ultimately successful, then the fate of this final social gathering place will be sealed.

There is one positive development within the village as grants have been secured to enable the village hall be to refurbished, so at least the villagers may be able to look forward to a future where they can have a place that might be seen as a centre for village functions.

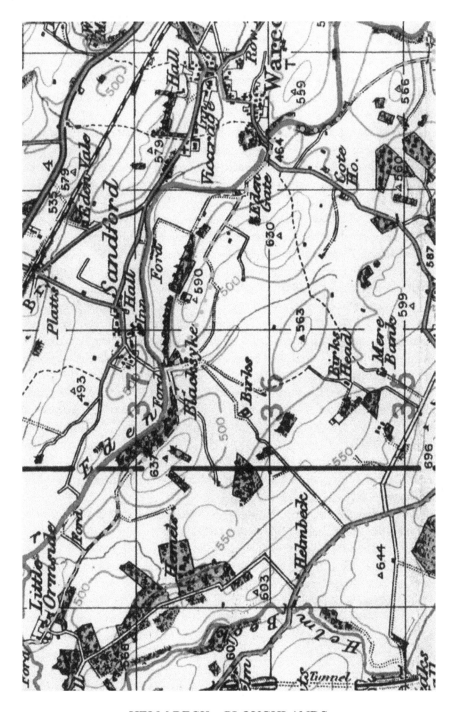

HELM BECK – PLOUGHLANDS

DAY NO. 9/MAP NO.5 PLOUGHLANDS – SOULBY

Leaving Warcop bridge, we follow a riverside path before joining Bermer Scar, a track that will lead us toward the farm at Ploughlands. A little way north of the buildings, where the track bifurcates, we follow the more southerly route before turning east to join Ploughlands Lane.

We don't stay on the track but turn south to follow Keldhead Sike across fields, joining the macadam road west of Little Musgrave, taking care to ensure that we stick to the path. Navigation continues to be slightly complicated to the south of the road as we cut across the fields to find Blind Beck leading to Sykeside from where it becomes Sykeside Lane and on to where it joins Mask Lane.

Mask Lane leads south into the delightful village of Soulby, where our day ends. AW had paddled in calf-deep water as he approached the Black Bull, where he sought overnight accommodation. The inn was one of two in the village but now both are gone; the Black Bull was demolished in the late 1960s and is now a grassed area. The Exchange Inn had closed prior to AW's visit, in 1935.

The history of Soulby in the twentieth century is not unlike that of Romaldkirk in so far as it had been a self-contained centre of commerce with shops, inns, cobblers, tailors etc. All are now gone but, like Romaldkirk, the village has maintained a close-knit sense of community. When AW visited, the Harvest Festival Sale was taking place in the village hall, a function that I was fortunate enough to be invited to when I first visited in 1998.

These traditions are the essence of village life, especially when chaired by a person such as Arthur Bainbridge, a well-known local man who, in 1998, had taken on the role of sale auctioneer for forty-nine years without a break. I had the pleasure of meeting this fine gentleman, who sadly died suddenly in 2000. Although AW was in the village on the evening of the sale, he chose not to attend for his mood was bleak, having found the customers and atmosphere of the inn not to his liking. In his account, he vividly describes the vulgar behaviour of a drinker by the name of Rowley.

Locals within the village recall 'Uncle Rowley' (Roland Fothergill), so called so as to distinguish him from his nephew Rowley (or Roland) Brass. He had come to live at Bridge End Farm and by 1938 was clearly a village 'character'. According to AW's account, Rowley attended the sale, believing it was his duty to help raise funds for the church. It seems that he also considered it his duty to be something of a boar.

AW refers to a raven-haired woman at the inn, who he grew to despise during the evening for her coarse appreciation of Rowley's stories. Details regarding Alice, her more elderly helper, are scant but the landlady was Margaret Morley, although the local older folk have few memories of her as custodian of the Black Bull.

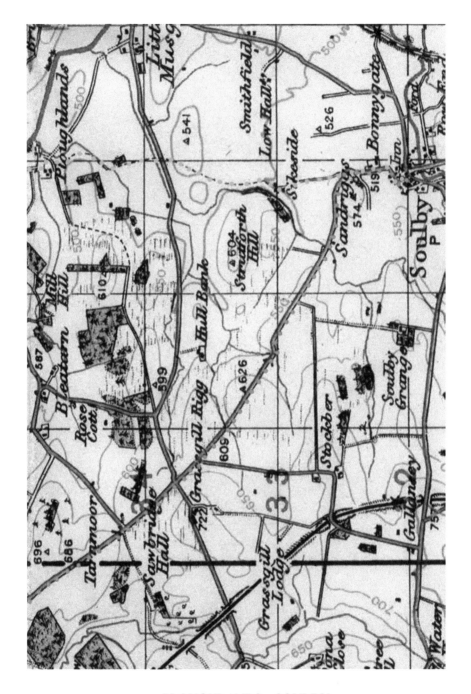

PLOUGHLANDS – SOULBY

DAY NO. 10

SOULBY TO DENT

DAY NO. 10

SOULBY TO DENT

O ur penultimate day sees us leaving the Eden valley and making our way over Waitby Common and Smardale Fell into the valley of the River Rawthey. A gradual descent towards Sedbergh, followed by skirting to the west of Frostrow, leads into Dentdale to join the Dales Way for the final stretch to Dent.

The day is divided into six legs as follows:

Leg	From:	To:
10 – 1	Soulby	Smardale Fell
10 – 2	Smardale Fell	Fat Lamb Inn
10 – 3	Fat Lamb Inn	Rawthey Bridge
10 – 4	Rawthey Bridge	Hebblethwaite
10 – 5	Hebblethwaite	Brackensgill
10 – 6	Brackensgill	Dent

The overall distance for the day's walk is approximately 21 miles on good tracks and roads in some cases, visiting two long distance paths; firstly we walk along part of the Coast to Coast path near Waitby and then end the day following the Dales Way in Dentdale.

We divert from AW for part of the day in avoiding the busy A683.

Two maps are required for the day from the 'Outdoor Leisure' series:

OL19   Howgill Fells and Upper Eden Valley

OL2   Yorkshire Dales (Southern & Western)

In requiring map OL2, we have now returned to the map with which we started our walk all those days ago and there is a great sense of achievement as we approach Dent, where the final map-change occurs.

Depending on the length of any breaks taken at the Fat Lamb Inn and Farfield Mill, it is best to allow 9 hours for the day's walk.

155

DAY NO. 10/MAP NO.1 SOULBY – SMARDALE FELL

When Arthur Bainbridge passed away, Soulby lost one of its fine characters. He was born and grew up in the village and attended the village school. Years later, after the school's closure, he was instrumental in instigating the use of the building for the community as a communal hall. It was at that hall that I had attended his forty-ninth chairing of the Festival Sale. He achieved one further before his untimely death.

On retirement, he started an activity that brought him renown outside the village environs. He began to build model buildings from pebbles and when I visited in 1998 his garden had become a veritable village of scaled-down properties. His labours were appreciated by all who saw them and he raised considerable sums for Cancer Research, but since his death the model village looks as though, sadly, it my die too.

While very much had changed in the years that had elapsed between AW's visit and my own, Arthur's own history was largely unchanged; when I visited him, he was still in the same house, Barney Scar, in which he had lived when AW was at Soulby. During his lifetime in the village, he witnessed first-hand the demise of the trades, the closure of both inns and the change from Soulby being a self-sufficient entity into a dormitory village.

Our way from Soulby follows the quiet single track road south toward Waitby. The road marks the end of the Eden valley and it was this return to more hilly topography that rejuvenated AW's flagging spirits and his enthusiasm and to forego his original thoughts of curtailing his trek at Kirkby Stephen and return by train.

Kirkby Stephen, like Appleby, was served by two railway stations in 1938 with the more central, Kirkby Stephen East, serving the line that was originally built to serve as a link between Barnard Castle and Tebay. Built to transport iron ore and coal to and from Cleveland, the Eden Valley Railway was a branch line northwards to Appleby and beyond. The branch actually evolved as the major route and the Tebay link was to close in 1952, ten years before the Eden Valley line. The line remained open until 1989 and served the military camp at Warcop before it too was closed.

AW's map shows a plethora of railways lines; the most southerly is the Settle–Carlisle line, originally built by the Midland Railway, later to become the London Midland and Scottish in 1923. The Eden Valley and the Tebay lines predate the more famous (and still running) competitor by fourteen years, opening in 1862.

Our way proceeds south along the quiet lane generally ascending towards Waitby, passing through the buttresses of the bridge of the Tebay line before passing under the Settle–Carlisle line. As we proceed south of the bridge we enjoy another association with AW's more recent contribution to long-distance walking when we join the Coast to Coast path. We encountered it briefly at Keld and we now follow it as we climb Smardale Fell.

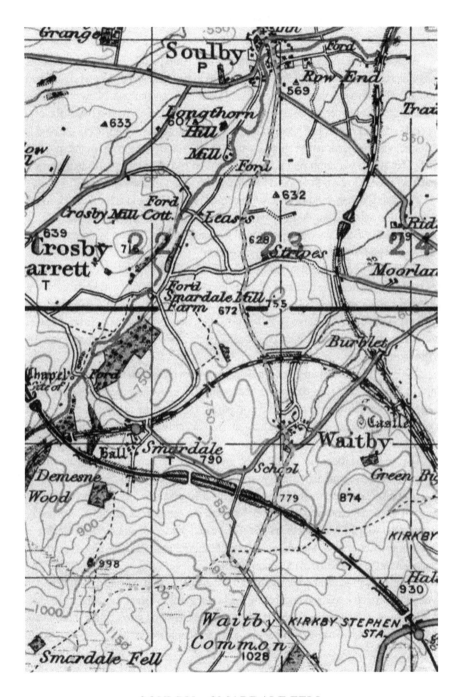

SOULBY – SMARDALE FELL

DAY NO. 10/MAP NO.2 SMARDALE FELL – FAT LAMB INN

We follow the Coast to Coast for a little less than a mile, when a bridleway leaves the long-distance route and heads south. The branch is to be found at the point where the two parallel walls turn south-west, with the Coast to Coast path continuing to follow the walls.

The bridleway proceeds generally southwards to join the main road between Ravenstonedale and Kirkby Stephen, close to a transmission mast. Turning left uphill the road is followed, thankfully, for only a short distance. There is little protection from the speeding traffic, but where we climb Ash Fell Ridge the road proceeds through a cutting and we make our way up to the right to join a footpath, which leads to a disused quarry.

The path generally follows the contours around Green Hill and at a crossroads in the paths we turn right, heading downhill on the track towards the buildings at Ash Fell. We are among a plethora of paths with the potential for confusion, but so long as we head south-east we will find our way ultimately to Bowber Head.

Finding our way to Bleaflatt, we will join Bleaflatt Lane, a quiet byway on which we are unlikely to be hounded by cars. Following the narrow lane for half a mile, we turn right at a road sign directing toward a camping site and follow Low Lane to Bowber Head and onwards to join the A683, turning right to follow the main road connecting Kirkby Stephen and Sedbergh, which is now the focus of our attention for it is toward Sedbergh that our route takes us.

AW's walk had seen him trek all the way south-west on this old turnpike for mile after mile. It is now a busy road connecting Sedbergh and Kirkby Stephen, and walking at its edge has little enjoyment to commend it to others. However, for the first stretch we can look forward to a break at the old coaching inn, the Fat Lamb Inn, which we will reach after half a mile.

The inn has a history that dates back to the origin of the turnpike, when main arterial routes of the late seventeenth century were upgraded and tolls would be charged for their use. Turnpike Trusts were established to operate these routes, which became the motorways of the seventeenth and eighteenth centuries. As commercial ventures, they finally began to fail with the arrival of the railways in the mid-nineteenth century and in the Local Government Act of 1888 the entire network of turnpike roads became disturnpiked and placed under the jurisdiction of the county councils.

The Fat Lamb Inn had originally been a coaching inn, with stabling and facilities for weary travelers, so it seems fitting that we might rest awhile. A short way south of the inn, AW's map shows a number 5. This is a numerical reference on the old map, showing the distance from Kirkby Stephen, whereas the new map simply shows 'MS'.

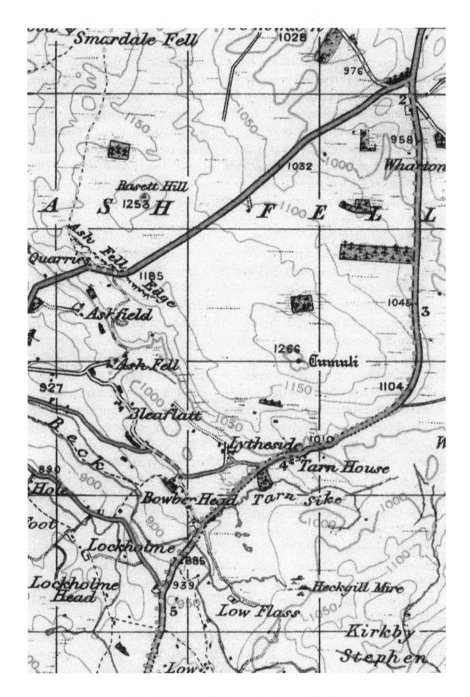

SMARDALE FELL – FAT LAMB INN

DAY NO. 10/MAP NO.3 FAT LAMB INN – RAWTHEY BRIDGE

We have no choice other than to continue on the roadside until the junction just north of milestone 6, as marked on AW's map. The road forks onto a pleasingly quieter lane at the stonework plinth, which would have housed milk churns back in the day.

This lane saves us two unpleasant miles of following the old turnpike road and we can savour a peaceful rural saunter, passing the intriguingly named 'Fell End Clouds'. The reference to the name 'clouds' in topographical features appears in a number of uplands hereabouts, such as Stennerskeugh Clouds and Clouds Gill. There is some debate over the origin of the word. It may have its root in the Anglo-Saxon word meaning 'clod', simply reflecting the knobbly nature of the ground underfoot; a second offering lies in terms used in earlier Celtic mining activity.

On the other side of the valley we are now passing the eastern edge of the Howgills and the different geology is very apparent. The clouds above us are formed from limestone, while the more rounded hill to the west, Harter Fell, is formed from a much earlier geological era and the reason for the significant difference lies in the valley below, which runs along the line of the Dent Fault. The fault line caused the land to the west to be lifted to a far greater extent than the limestone to the east and the subsequent glacial action has created differential erosion and the scenery that we see today.

In my explanation of how to use this guide, I indicated that any grid reference used refers to modern maps and any gridlines in the AW maps should be ignored. This section is a good example of how the OS have changed the reference grids to what we know now.

It is only at the beginning of the twentieth century that gridlines became the norm and the reference numbers on the grids were part of a larger national grid that gave co-ordinates for any particular place as an alphanumeric reference. This grid would have been in place on the maps that AW used which, in 1938, would have been the 'Popular Edition'. A new edition had been planned but there then occurred three events that altered the direction of the OS's output. The first was the 1936 retriangulation, the second was the report commissioned in 1935 with the Davidson Committee enquiry looking into the role of the OS in the twentieth century and finally the outbreak of war in 1939.

The combined result was the 'War Series' of OS maps using the original gridlines, with a new grid datum only introduced after the war in what we know as OSGB36, based on the retriangulation that took place between 1936 and 1962 and also incorporating the Davidson Committee Report findings published in 1938. This new series was known as the 'New Popular Edition largely based on the original 'Popular Edition'.

Our tranquil walk continues along the lane, passing what was marked as 'Foggygill School' but is now a tractor supplier, and on to join the main road at Rawthey Bridge.

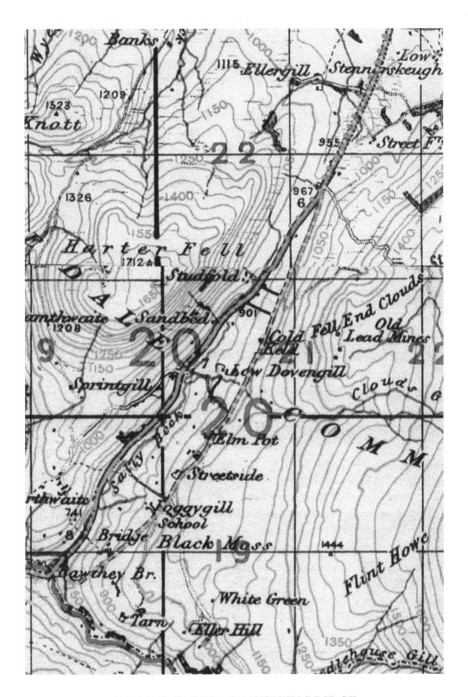

FAT LAMB INN – RAWTHEY BRIDGE

DAY NO. 10/MAP NO.4 RAWTHEY BRIDGE – HEBBLETHWAITE

On crossing the River Rawthey, we enter the Yorkshire Dales National Park and will remain within its boundaries until our journey's end. The park was created in 1954 and understandably was contained with the confines of Yorkshire. We have seen how in 1974 the Local Government Act had redrawn the boundaries of Westmorland and Cumberland to form Cumbria but also this new incomer claimed parts of what had previously been the North and West Ridings of Yorkshire.

We shall remain in Cumbria until having ascended Deepdale, south of Dentdale, yet for all those miles we will be within the national park boundary, such was the encroachment of the new county.

Immediately beyond Rawthey Bridge a track leads off to the south-west, following a rough path skirting Bluecaster Fell. Until 1819, this track was the turnpike route, but it was rerouted to easier slopes and the new route took it past what is now the Cross Keys Inn. The inn is visible as we proceed toward Bluecaster Side, but if you have a fancy for a pint then I fear this is not the place for you, for not a drop of alcohol is on sale. The Cross Keys is a temperance inn and is owned by the National Trust.

The inn wasn't originally a coaching inn but was a farm known as High Haygarth (the maps refer to 'Low Haygarth' suggesting that there once would have been a higher version). Although it has remained as an inn since that time it came into the ownership of a Mrs Edith Bunney in 1902, who removed the liquor licence and ran it as a temperance inn. On her death in 1949, her will bequeathed the inn to the National Trust, which stipulated that it should remain unlicensed.

Beyond Bluecaster Side the track becomes a firmer surfaced lane and after a short distance a path leads off to the right, which descends to join the main road at High Wardses farm. Next to the farm our route is to follow the access track down to the river. Our progress down the Rawthey valley now follows a series of paths, which aren't always easy to follow but so long as that progress is generally downstream then all will be well.

Initially we follow the eastern side of the river as far as Beck Side, where after a short distance we can cross the river and turn south to follow a grassy path to Brow Side. Beyond Brow Side the path bends east to recross the river, but we turn slightly west to follow south on a bridleway that runs the length of the valley. The bridleway generally follows the contours of the western side of the valley and proceeds to the next buildings at Fawcett Bank. At this point on AW's map, the thick black line is part of the magnetic north pointer that, in 1942, indicated that grid north was in excess of 11 degrees east of magnetic north. By 1997, this had decreased to only 5 degrees so we can presumably look forward to navigating being much easier as midway through the twenty-first century grid and magnetic north will coincide.

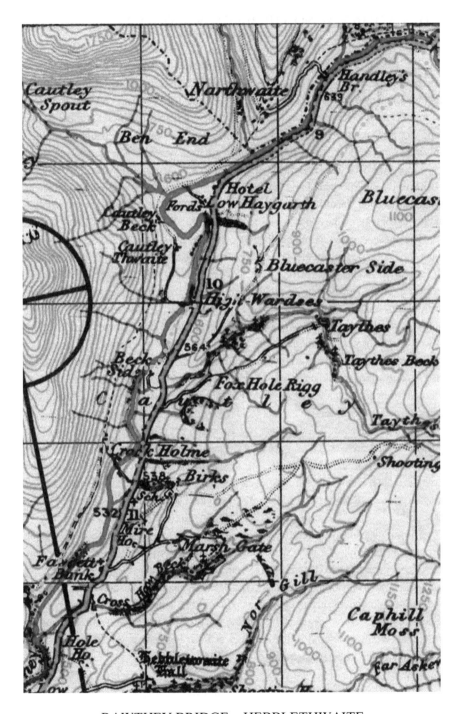

RAWTHEY BRIDGE – HEBBLETHWAITE

DAY NO. 10/MAP NO.5 HEBBLETHWAITE – BRACKENSGILL

This section of the day's walk joins a part of another long-distance walk that we have encountered before on the first day. The Dales Way follows the entire length of Dentdale and we join it near Sedbergh at the dale's western end. The bridleway on the western side of the Rawthey valley continues to Thursgill, where it begins to become a more formal lane. For all that, though, it remains a very pleasant walk to the next buildings at Ellerthwaite following Buckbank Lane to reach the farm from which the lane takes its name.

From Buckbank there is a choice of ways, with the route shown by me as continuing south-west along Buckbank Lane. It is possible to follow a path through the farm buildings to join a riverside walk to Straight Bridge and beyond to New Bridge then, crossing the bridge, to continue on the opposite bank to the hamlet of Millthrop to join the Dales Way.

The principle reason for my not following the river route is that it has been a long walk since the Fat Lamb Inn and there is nowhere for refreshment other than the Weavers Café at Farfield Mill on the banks of the River Clough. The mill is now a heritage and arts centre, opened in 2004 following major refurbishment from its previous derelict state. It had originally begun wool spinning in 1837 and was still noted as such on AW's map.

The yarn from the mill was used in the Sedbergh and Dent knitting industries and it saw 100 years of wool spinning until the Second World War when it became a manufacturing centre of aircraft parts. After the war, it never again returned to full production, but had a variety of uses until finally fully closing in 1992. In the late 1990s, the buildings were rescued by the local building preservation trust and it is they who ultimately secured funding to finance the renovation of the mill buildings.

Leaving Farfield, we could find our way back to the river to follow the route above but I chose to head more directly toward Millthrop and Dentdale. Passing the cottages at the entrance to the Farfield Mill complex, we follow the lane to the left along to its junction with the main road to Sedbergh. Taking care, we make our way to and then along the unclassified lane until we arrive at Millthrop and join the Dales Way for the remainder of the day.

The track leading away from the village climbs to skirt around the western slopes of the Frostrow Fells. While we have seen many changes between 1938 and the present day, these have generally reflected changes in commercial or industrial activity; however, we now pass over land that was part of the 'original' Sedbergh Golf Course. When AW passed the course shows on his map as extending up Long Rigg. It has since been abandoned and a new nine-hole course opened in 1991 in the valley of the River Dee that is opening up before us. We then descend to the buildings at Rash before crossing the river at Rash Bridge to then follow the southern side of the valley.

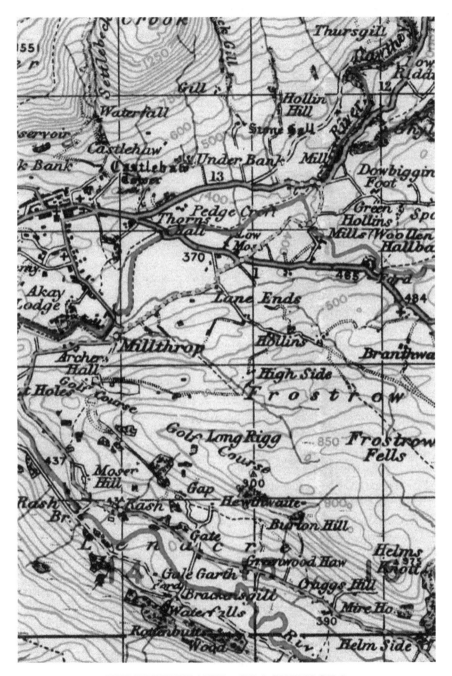

HEBBLETHWAITE – BRACKENSGILL

DAY NO. 10/MAP NO.6 BRACKENSGILL – DENT

The eagle-eyed map-reader will notice that the route map around Rash Bridge does not reflect the modern directions for the Dales Way. The main reason for the divergence is that, back in the 1990s, crossing the Dee at Rash Bridge was the route; however, from time to time, the route has been amended for various reasons and this was one such change. The recent building of the Brackensgill footbridge has given us a choice to make.

The Dales Way was originally (but unofficially, as it was not then a recognised national trail for inclusion on the OS maps of the time) opened in 1969 and it is evident that AW had considered using at least part of it for his own project of devising a route from coast to coast. After many years in an unhappy marriage, which was presumably held together so as not to damage his social standing, after retirement AW and his first wife, Ruth, divorced. In 1970 he remarried (Betty) and honeymooned in York. He wrote to a friend that the walking was not at all bad and that he might use parts of other walks to complete his coast-to-coast trek. One of the walks referred to was the Dales Way.

It is hard to imagine from AW's description of his progress into Dentdale in 1938 that he would ever want to visit the dale again. His commentary is less than inspiring, with the only thing worse than his own depression being that of the weather, with continued gales, rain and hail. AW had been dogged with appalling weather for the previous few days and it may be purely coincidental that two weeks before his encounter with such foul conditions the north-eastern seaboard of the USA was hit by the severest hurricane since the mid-nineteenth century. The 1938 'Long Island Express', as it was dubbed, was the most expensive ever experienced, only beaten in 2012 by Hurricane Sandy. It is often said that what strikes America will strike the UK some days later.

He continued for what seemed like an interminable distance east and finally arrived in Dent, remarking that he felt that it was 'not of this world'. He was initially scathing about the place, liking it to being a nightmare where Blanchland was like a dream. He became melancholy too about how his escapade was nearly over and that he had to return to a life of rules and regulations.

AW witnessed Dent as it neared the end of its association with a cottage industry that had been at its heart for hundreds of years – knitting. The village (or perhaps that should be town, for until 1863 it was known as Dent Town, being the administrative centre for the dale, a role then taken over by Sedbergh) has long been associated with the 'terrible knitters of Dent'. Entire families would eke out a meagre existence through the knitting of hosiery, the yarn for which was generally supplied from mills such as Farfield Mill and other spinning mills close to Sedbergh.

AW found lodgings with Mr and Mrs Mason for the night and Mrs Mason spent the entire evening rhythmically knitting 'as regular as the ticking of the clock'.

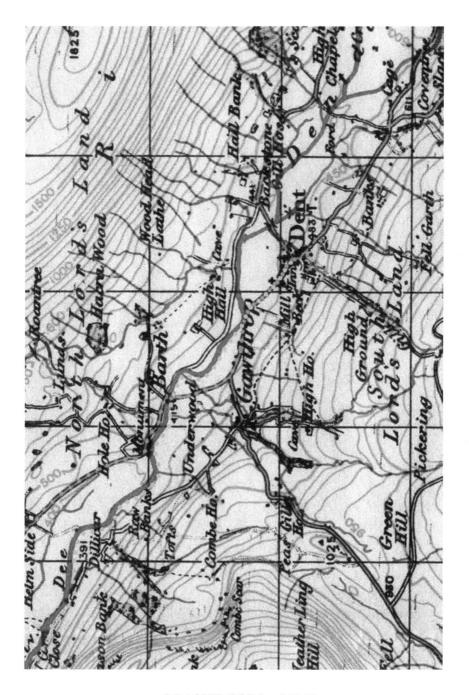

BRACKENSGILL – DENT

DAY NO. 11

DENT TO SETTLE

DAY NO. 11

DENT TO SETTLE

With one final slog up Deepdale, serious hill climbs are complete. The route then follows Kingsdale, a most peaceful and little-visited dale that most will not have heard of. From the isolation of Kingsdale we then have a total change of human pace as we join the handbag walkers at the Ingleton Falls Walk.

Ingleton provides a fascinating history associated with the railways and gives an interesting proposition relating to a famous literary figure. The literary connection continues as we proceed towards Clapham and the walking becomes easier as we follow the southern edge of the higher limestone hills.

Our final climb is encountered beyond Feizor before beginning the descent into Ribblesdale and down to what had been our starting point all those days before. Our adventure will end where it began, in Settle.

This final day is split into seven legs as follows:

Leg	From:	To:
11 – 1	Dent	Deepdale
11 – 2	Deepdale	Kingsdale
11 – 3	Kingsdale	Ingleton
11 – 4	Ingleton	Newby
11 – 5	Newby	Clapham
11 – 6	Clapham	Austwick
11 – 7	Austwick	Settle

The total distance for the day is in the order of 22 miles, with the first three legs providing nothing by way of refreshment breaks. Once we arrive at Ingleton, we will find civilisation with tea rooms, inns and shops and as this is approximately half-distance it will provide a suitable lunch stop.

The second half of the walk will give choices for breaks at Clapham and Austwick, and at the time of writing there exists a delightful tea room in the hamlet of Feizor.

Although most of today's walking can be found on one OS 'Outdoor Leisure' series map there is a short section from the west of Feizor where our route will be found on OL41 (Forest of Bowland and Ribblesdale). I have concluded that this is such a short section with little by way of navigation problems that the purchase (and carrying) of a further map is not merited. The map needed for this final day is, therefore:

OL2   Yorkshire Dales (Southern & Western)

DAY NO. 11/MAP NO.1 DENT – DEEPDALE

It's interesting how our impression of a place or a person can be affected by a bit of sunshine or a kindly act by a stranger. So was AW's perception of Dent and Dentdale influenced by the morning that dawned bright and also by the kindliness of Mr Mason who had, unasked, set to and repaired a sole-fixing nail in AW's rapidly deteriorating boots.

In his initial account of his journey, AW espoused his appreciation of Mr Mason's action having been carried out without request. Fifty years later, in writing the narrative for Wainwright in the Limestone Dales, he reminisced on the same events of 1938 and wrote that his host had 'roused himself at my request to hammer a protruding nail'. Whichever version is correct is something of a formality; the key fact was that his impression of Dent had changed from his damning judgement of the previous evening.

Joseph Mason was a local man having been born a little way up the tributary valley of Deepdale and we will pass his family home, believed to be at Hill Top Farm as related to me by an elderly resident, May (never discovered her surname), of the village who remembered the Masons. She recalled him at work just as AW had described at a time when Dent, like so many other rural communities, provided for all the services that might be necessary for its residents.

In the 1930s, Dent boasted five inns and three banks among forty-seven businesses and twenty shops along the main street. Today, as we have seen elsewhere, such services are to be found only in larger towns leaving the tourists to trek from one trinket shop to another. There remains a well-stocked general store and post office along with a heritage museum and tourist information centre. In a twist of commercial fate the museum has been opened on the site of what had once been the village filling station in earlier years.

Wainwright in the Limestone Dales is significant for another, rather sadder reason; it being published just two months after AW's death in 1991. It is evident that he had penned the words for the book sometime earlier, for in his general comments surrounding Dent he bemoans the loss of the individuality of the village, it having been destroyed by the coming of the motor car. He concluded that he 'liked Dent better fifty years ago', a clear reference to his visit back in 1938.

In leaving Dent our route, perhaps slavishly, follows AW's original route and it should be pointed out that there does exist an alternative using the path up Flintergill heading generally south. The path follows the gill as part of the Flintergill Outrake Nature Trail and is likely be busy with day trippers, for it forms part of a well-trodden circuit walk for those who have parked their cars down in the village. AW himself passed this way in his 1970 book Walks in Limestone Country and walkers would be 'too far gone if they cannot manage this, and even further gone if they cannot enjoy every yard of it'.

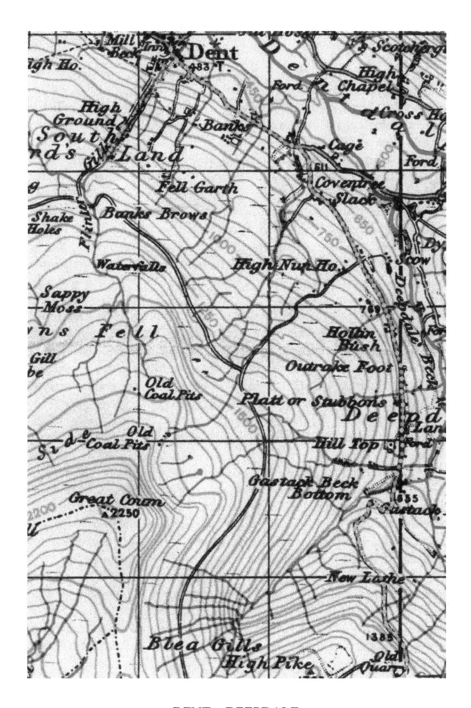

DENT – DEEPDALE

DAY NO. 11/MAP NO.2 DEEPDALE – KINGSDALE

If you have decided to follow the Flintergill route, you will finally rejoin the AW route at the southern end of Deepdale close to the dale's watershed with Kingsdale.

The road that branches off the Dent to Lea Yeat road and ascends as Deepdale Lane up the western slopes of the dale was described by AW as a narrow rutted lane between scented hedgerows. It remains a little-used byway with few cars to spoil the walk. AW's reference to the ruts clearly relates to what was often the state of such rural roads. In his book The Story of the Yorkshire Dales, W. R. Mitchell confirms that the road was only macadamed shortly after the Second World War, some years after AW passed along it.

The road continues to the watershed at White Shaw Moss and as it nears the highest point of the road the junction to the right is the green lane known as Occupation Road. If you have chosen to use the alternative Flintergill route, then it is along this lane that the route will rejoin the road route. Kingsdale now lies ahead and we very soon leave Cumbria and find ourselves back in Yorkshire (even though we have been in the Yorkshire Dales National Park since early on Day 10).

In AW's account, he described Kingsdale's river, known as Kingsdale Beck, in the tranquil upper reaches of the dale before it becomes the River Twiss as it tumbles in a much more lively fashion downhill on its way to its confluence with the River Doe at Ingleton. He noted that it seemed "to have been engineered, like an irrigation ditch or a canal'. His observation was very near the truth, for Kingsdale Beck is indeed an engineered waterway and it was canalised as part of the enclosure of the valley.

The enclosures refer to various government enclosure acts in which previously common land was brought into use for agriculture, with many of the field boundaries that we see today dating from this time.

There is some question as to whether the beck was canalised at the time of the 1819 enclosure. The terms of the enclosure included reference to 'provision is made for the "public Watercourse called Kingsdale Beck" to be kept open, cleansed and scoured and kept in its present Course'. This suggests that the beck had been straightened prior to the proposed enclosure. Careful observation of the valley floor shows evidence of the original course of the beck as it meandered along the flat valley floor.

AW also referred to the caves within the dale, the most famous of which is the cave known as Yordas Cave. This was a favourite Victorian show cave that was firmly on the tourist trail, with stone steps carved at its entrance. In his later book Walks in Limestone Country (1970), AW included a walk that incorporated the cave and he set aside a page to describe its main features. He pondered on the habit of the Nordic Giant, Yordas, after whom the cave was named, to eat small boys – AW wondered 'why not small girls?'

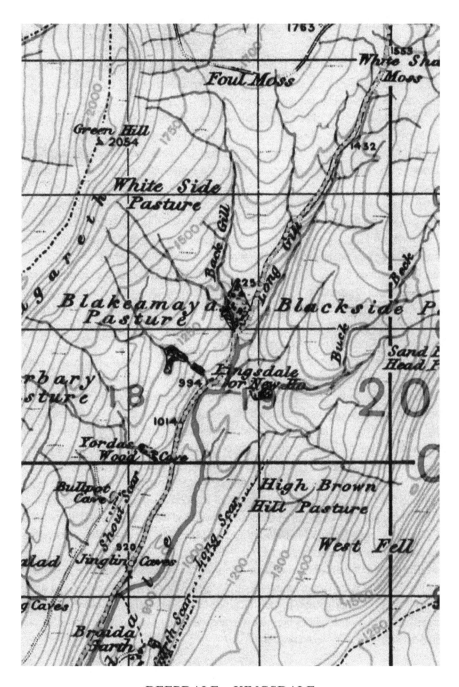

DEEPDALE – KINGSDALE

DAY NO. 11/MAP NO.3 KINGSDALE – INGLETON

We leave the solitude of Kingsdale with its two dwellings (being the farms of Braida Garth and Kingsdale Head) to join the tourists thronging along the course of the River Twiss as they marvel at the famous Ingleton Falls.

Before leaving the U-shaped glaciated valley we are faced with the sight of the dale having no obvious outlet, it being surrounded on all four sides by higher ground suggesting that the valley once contained a lake. If it did then the lake's waters found an exit route through erosion of the Raven Ray terminal moraine at the southern extremity of the dale's glacial activity.

We follow the valley road to an obvious green track leading off left between walls, and after crossing the footbridge over the beck we ascend Raven Ray before finding the path to the right that leads down to the bridge of what is now shown on the OS map as the River Twiss. We are now on the Ingleton Waterfalls Trail and can follow it all the way into Ingleton. It is very likely that we will cease to enjoy the solitude that has been ours in Kingsdale.

In AW's 1970 account in Walks in Limestone Country, his words and sketches refer to the river being the Doe with the River Greta as the eastern of the two watercourses flowing toward Ingleton. The modern map shows the rivers as the Twiss and the Doe with the River Greta commencing at the confluence of the two.

The walks were officially opened in 1885 and the confusion over the names of the rivers seems to continue to this day. In his later book Wainwright in the Limestone Dales, AW makes reference to the contention over the names recalling that when he was young the western river was known as the Doe and the eastern the Twiss. He refers to the confusion that seemed to reign at the OS as they switched the names and then changed the eastern beck to the Greta (the name by which the river is known as on the map opposite which is presumably the map used by AW in preparing his map in his guide).

Marie Hartley and Joan Ingilby's comments in their 1956 book The Yorkshire Dales continue to confirm the longstanding nature of the query regarding the rivers' names. Whilst they agree that the rivers are indeed the Twiss and the Doe they assert that it is the Twiss that flows from Chapel-le-Dale and the Doe from Kingsdale so AW's memory from his younger days appears substantiated.

The descent of the Twiss valley ends at the visitor centre and as we arrive at the road we turn left toward the village centre. As we do, the old railway viaduct can be seen spanning the valley of what has now become the River Greta and we climb up onto Main Street and into the heart of delightful Ingleton. We are something close to half-distance on our final day so a lunch stop would be well-advised.

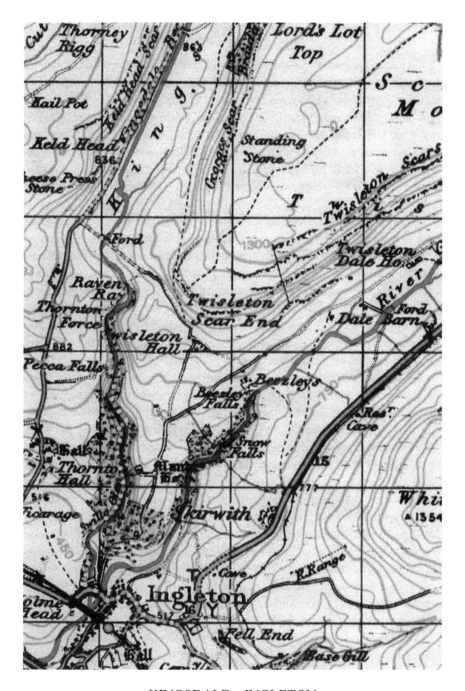

KINGSDALE – INGLETON

DAY NO. 11/MAP NO.4 INGLETON – NEWBY

It is hard to imagine Ingleton presenting anything other than a centre for tourism with its tea rooms and gift shops. The evidence that the village has an industrial heritage can only really be seen in the viaduct that crosses the valley of the infant River Greta.

In 1938, as AW passed through, Ingleton had seen the demise of its coal-mining industry just one year earlier. In 1937, the New Ingleton Colliery, built adjacent to the A65, ceased production and the last of the pits in the small coalfield around Ingleton closed. This pit had opened as late as 1913 and had been sufficiently productive to have seen an influx of miners, requiring the construction of housing, the result being the planned estate known as 'New Village'.

It is somewhat unfortunate that the miners' work underground was the cause of subsidence to the housing in New Village that had been built for them. The huge cost of rectification was a contributory factor in the ultimate cessation of the work that had provided the livelihood of the very men who lived in them. Paradoxically, Ingleton also suffered many years earlier with the construction of the railway. The coming of the railway to Ingleton tells a story of squabbling between companies, each of whom put their own profits above the needs of the customers. In the days of pioneering nineteenth-century railway construction there were a number of individual private concerns vying for business with little or no cohesion between them.

The start of the farcical story begins with the proposed railway link between West Yorkshire and Scotland and the North Western Railway commenced construction, only to find that escalating costs required a major alteration to the route. This resulted in Ingleton, from 1849, being the terminus of the line from the junction at Clapham. By this stage, though, the viaduct foundations were in place, remaining redundant beyond the buffers of the station. In 1850 the line was abandoned as the main route ran more southerly toward Lancaster.

The Midland Railway resurrected the line in 1861 with a view to securing the shortest route to Scotland. However, the long-running animosity between the two companies ultimately meant that, in their refusal to cooperate, a second, separate station was built at Thornton at the northern end of the viaduct. This inability to coexist even led to totally separate services, the timetables of which did not coincide with travellers having to manhandle their baggage from one station to the next. In 1923, railway reorganisation merged the companies to form the London, Midland and Scottish Railway and finally, after sixty years, the Thornton halt was removed from the timetables and subsequently demolished.

Our route from Ingleton follows Old Road before following the minor road to Cold Cotes, then crossing field paths to find the track into the village of Newby.

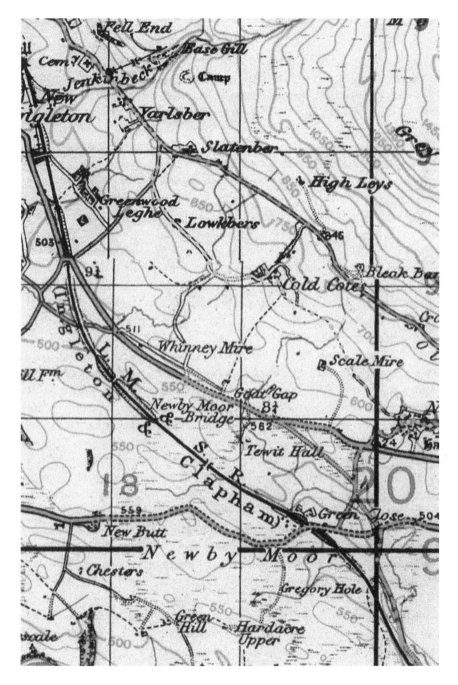

INGLETON – NEWBY

DAY NO. 11/MAP NO.5 NEWBY – CLAPHAM

Our way takes us through the hamlet of Newby to find a track leading eastwards (do not take the first signposted path, the track being a short distance further along the road). The track leads back to the old road connecting Ingleton and Clapham. Turning right on this quiet byway will lead us to the pleasant village of Clapham and we begin a series of literal coincidences.

The first relates to the possible origin of a very famous detective; the second revisits a literary giant to whom we have already encountered on Day 1; the third refers to the early beginnings for what to many a Yorkshireman has become part of the very nature of being Yorkshire.

The detective connection is borne out of the fact that Mary Doyle came to reside in Thornton in 1883. In 1876 there had occurred the tragic death at Ingleton station of one Randall Hopley Sherlock, who had a window in the local church dedicated to him, along with a commemorative plaque. Mrs Doyle's son, Arthur Conan Doyle, was a regular visitor to the area in the years prior to the first publication of his famous sleuth stories. Perhaps it is mere coincidence, but with the region under the viaduct being known as 'The Holmes', it seems reasonable to conclude that Ingleton may hold the answer to the mystery of the origin of the detective's name.

On the first day of our trek, we witnessed the fact that J. B. Priestley has a continuing connection with Hubberholme Church as his ashes are interred there (his book An English Journey, published in 1936, was perhaps itself an influencing factor of AW's choice of title). It seems fitting that Priestley has a very definite connection with Clapham, for he was the first contributor in the inaugural edition of the Yorkshire Dalesman, our third coincidence. In the magazine, Priestley described his love of Yorkshire's hills and valleys, adding: 'So please see that your new magazine fights to keep them all unspoilt.'

The Yorkshire Dalesman was first published in an unassuming house that was also the home of Harry Scott, a journalist at the Craven Herald. In 1935, he came to live at Fellside in Clapham and was keen to establish a periodical magazine that would be aimed at Dales folk. He achieved publication just a matter of months after AW's trek, with the first edition going on sale in April 1939. The magazine is read around the globe and has undoubtedly helped to maintain the profile of the Dales and keep them unspoilt, as Priestley had wished. In reflecting its wider coverage, the magazine's name was changed to the Dalesman in 1948 and still thrives today.

In Clapham, after arriving along Eggshell Lane, our way turns along Riverside and follows the lane to the left past the church. The track proceeds through the Ingleborough Hall tunnels and on to Thwaite Lane, heading east towards Austwick.

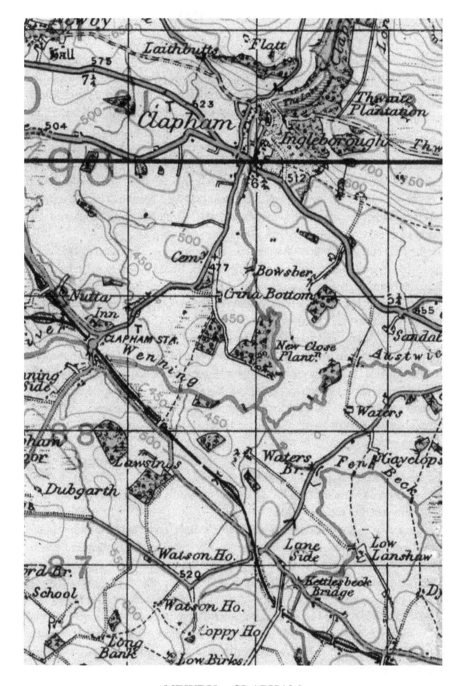

NEWBY – CLAPHAM

DAY NO. 11/MAP NO.6 CLAPHAM – AUSTWICK

Thwaite Lane has been a thoroughfare for many years and the tunnels through which we have passed were constructed in the pursuit of increased privacy for the Victorian owners of Ingleborough Hall. The Farrer family had owned the estate from the late eighteenth century and remodeled much of the northern end of the village, including constructing the dam to form the Ingleborough Lake in the 1840s.

A spectacular tour of the grounds was available to visitors accessing the 'back garden' by crossing the dam and on via Clapdale Drive to Trow Gill and Clapdale Cave (now Ingleborough Show Cave), which had been made accessible in 1837. The most renowned member of the Farrer family was Reginald, born in 1880, who became an intrepid traveller, searching out new botanic species from far and wide. The exotic plants he returned with would adorn the valley of the Fell Back to the eastern side of the lake.

Reginald only lived until 1920 when, on a trip to Burma, he contracted diphtheria and died in the absence of adequate medical treatment. The Farrers moved from the hall in the 1930s and after spells as an evacuee centre during the Second World War, it became a residential school before finally being developed into an outdoor activity facility for local authority schools in the 1970s.

Trow Gill became famous for more than just part of a grandiose garden tour when, in 1947, male human remains were found hidden in a cave by two potholers. The subsequent postmortem failed to identify the deceased, but showed that he had died between two and six years prior, and that among his possessions was a small ampule of powder identified as sodium cyanide. There followed a locally generated assumption that he was a German spy but this was never unequivocally established. However, the story of the Trow Gill skeleton remains a mystery.

Thwaite Lane continues until it reaches Townhead Lane, where, turning right, we follow the quiet road down into the village of Austwick. Austwick's local history tells of a village with predominantly agricultural roots and the area is surrounded by pastoral farmland with a variety of breeds of cattle.

The area was, at the time of Reginald Farrer's death, home to an establishment that might have saved his life. The hospital shown on AW's map was the Harden Bridge Isolation Hospital, which was opened in 1907 to provide medical facilities for infectious diseases such as diphtheria and scarlet fever. Many of the patients were transferred from the Giggleswick workhouse, which had been deemed too close to neighbouring properties to house such a facility. The Harden Bridge unit went on to become a convalescent hospital before closing in 1991. In an ironic twist, many of its patients were transferred to Castlebergh Hospital in Giggleswick, which had been the very workhouse that many had originally been transferrerd from.

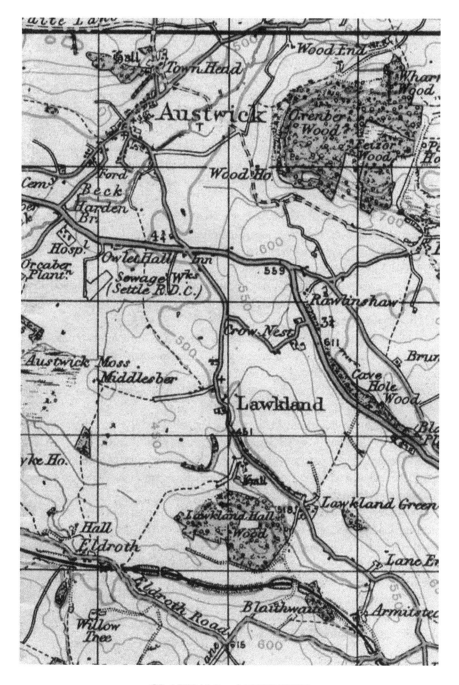

CLAPHAM – AUSTWICK

DAY NO. 11/MAP NO.7 AUSTWICK – SETTLE

We have walked many miles together but now find ourselves on the last lap, with around 3 miles remaining. The first part of this final leg comprises an easy stroll from Austwick along the green lane, crossing Wood Lane and proceeding south along Hale Lane toward Wood House.

It is at this point that our route leaves the southern edge of the Outdoor Leisure OS map and if we are to have modern map coverage of our walk we will need Ordnance Survey OL41. We will find our way back onto OL2 after approximately 1 mile of 'blind' walking but as the navigation is straightforward the purchase of another map for such a short distance is not merited.

Hale Lane is a pleasant green track that leads all the way into the hamlet of Feizor. AW's account did not comment on these final villages of our journey, for his route from Newby had followed a more southerly course, largely along roads passing Clapham Station and Eldroth.

Our route leaves Feizor at the track heading south-east, adjacent to the shallow ford. The track is followed for approximately half a mile to where it begins to turn south, where we fork left on a less well-defined path.

We have walked many miles to see the Roman wall yet here, just two miles from where we set out, we can find a wall even older than Hadrian's. Known locally as the 'Celtic Wall', it was described in AW's Walks in Limestone Country and he commented that it was not included on the OS map. It remains an omission from the maps but can be found at 802675, which is slightly off our route but worthy of a detour.

It seems fitting to visit another ancient wall, although this one is very much smaller than that visited earlier on our trek. The history of the 'Celtic Wall' is unclear but it certainly looks to be something more than just the remnant of a field boundary. Shown on the map near to the wall is Dead Man's Cave but, unlike the cave in Trow Gill, there is no association with murder or death.

Our route follows south-east towards the hamlet of Stackhouse where, just short of the buildings, the path forks and we follow the southerly path with our destination now directly ahead. The path skirts around Lord's Wood and finally the way underfoot becomes macadamed. We join the main road and turn left where, in after a matter of yards, we will walk past the end of the path that we set out on eleven days before.

We have walked more than 200 miles, from Yorkshire through Durham, Northumberland, Cumbria and back to Yorkshire. We have walked through a huge expanse of history all in our aim of following in AW's footsteps.

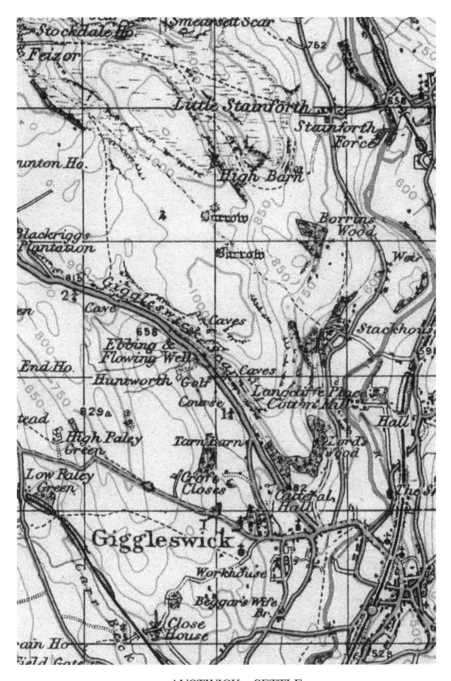

AUSTWICK – SETTLE

IN WAINWRIGHT'S FOOTSTEPS

CONCLUSION

IN WAINWRIGHT'S FOOTSTEPS

CONCLUSION

The maps within this section of the guide are thankfully not be to be walked unless you have a desire to savour such displeasure as AW had experienced all those years earlier. He had been distinctly unimpressed and it is fair to assume that modern traffic would render retreading this way as sheer lunacy.

In copying the maps that accommodate the route chosen by AW, I concluded it might be acceptable to end this guide on a light-hearted note and in so doing I have included some quotes from AW from his account of the journey. I have also included some extracts of my own account which, like AW's narrative, have lain in a drawer for many years and no doubt will remain so for the foreseeable future.

The maps refer to those sections of AW's walk that commenced in Leadgate with his decision to steer clear of Cross Fell at the start of the eighth day. He then proceeded westwards up to the Hartside Pass along the road that he noted was a gradual incline but on the ascent he satisfied himself with the thought that he 'had never witnessed a mountain in a blacker mood than Cross Fell on that October Sabbath'.

However wise it may have been in 1938 to keep to the road, I have suggested in my Day 8 guide that with modern walking equipment and a well-defined path, there should be no difficulties. The crossing of Fiend's Fell (as Cross Fell had been known in years gone by) is certainly one of the highpoints that remains in my memory of my escape to the country. To be fair to AW he could not rely on the clear waymarking of the path that became the Pennine Way; this has undoubtedly made the crossing a safer proposition than it might once have been.

Although I had been retracing his trek, it may be argued that I am not being true to his route. As a counter to this assertion, it is perhaps adequate to quote from my own manuscript in which, like AW, I wrote an account of my journey: 'I had thought long and hard about the spirit of my adventure, vis-à-vis whether the route should be over or around Cross Fell. I had satisfied myself that although I was parting company with the man I was following my route-plan only accommodated what he had wished but did not dare attempt in the adverse weather.'

However straightforward the route over Cross Fell might be, I am reminded of a less-than-successful walk some years prior with my wife, Sue: 'I maintained that we would not have erred were it not for the break in my navigational concentration as a direct result of being shouted at for being a total moron for having suggested such a walk in the first place. Sue continues to maintain that whatever my excuses might be I was still a total moron for having suggested such a walk in the first place. At the time I consoled her by assuring her that we were not lost, we simply were not where we should have been. She inquired in shrill scream as to what the hell was the difference.'

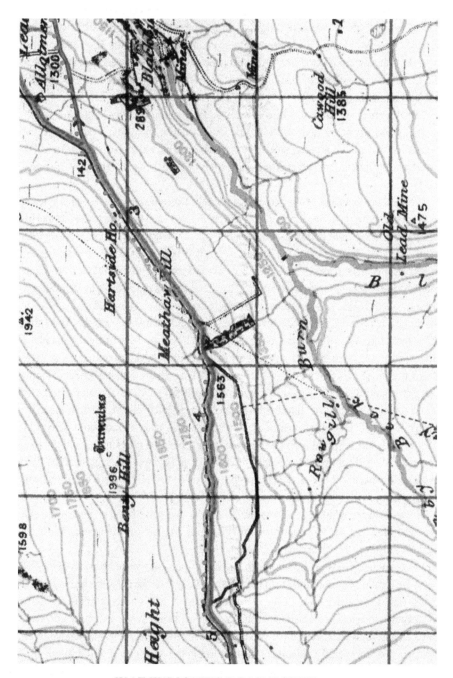

WAINWRIGHT'S ROAD ROUTE

AW's wet and windy trudge continued up to Hartside Cross and he referred in his account to the café at Hartside Top, which lays a reasonable claim to being the highest café in England. Beyond Hartside Top, the steep descent into the Eden valley begins and as the road skirts the slopes of Gamblesby Allotments he gave up the ghost and sought refuge at the Red Lion in the village of Gamblesby. His intention was to restart his day's walk if the weather improved.

The weather, which we have already seen was being influenced by severe Atlantic depressions, did not relent and he had no option other than to overnight at the inn. His description of the inn is accurate and its location can be easily found, but sadly there will be no young lady looking to attend to our needs for it is no more and Gamblesby has no hostelry.

There is no doubt that AW's account is generally accurate in its relating of his trek and in one passage within his recollection of his stay at the Red Lion he refers to the fact that his 'favourite football team had been defeated yesterday by four goals to one, and were deposed from the leadership of the league'. AW had been a founding member of the Blackburn Rovers supporters' club, so it is clear to which team that he refers. In checking the historical football fixtures, it is true that Blackburn Rovers did lose 4-1 to Millwall and, having been top of the league, dropped to second place as a result of the defeat.

In passing over Hartside, AW had reached an altitude that was 1,000 feet lower than the summit of Cross Fell, so it can only be imagined how foul the conditions would have been at the higher altitude. I was suffering my own problems, having opted to take on Cross Fell. My own account refers to a howling east wind and perhaps, with the benefit of knowledge only gained subsequently, I had encountered a Helm wind. As a wearer of glasses I was certainly struggling with how best to be able to map-read in the driving rain:'When the matter of my not being able to see through my glasses was taken into account I was beginning to think that a helpful solution might be to run about the plateau in ever decreasing circles shouting "Don't panic". Resisting the startling simplicity of this suggestion I arrived at the conclusion that it was essential to restore my vision to a point where I could actually see something.'

I was fortunate in finding the cross-wall shelter on the summit and on its leeward side was able to collect my thoughts, clean my glasses and regain my composure to set out again in a distinctly hostile environment.

At Gamblesby, AW ended his eighth day in the splendour of the bedroom at the Red Lion. He recalled the room thus: '"In the very middle of the room was the bed, a few minutes' walk from where I stood'. An interesting aspect of AW's account of his stay at the inn relates to the fact that he paid 'eight shillings for tea, supper, a heavenly bed, and breakfast'. At the time of writing these concluding comments I calculate that, allowing for inflation, this amounts to a current cost somewhere in the order of £23. Little wonder that we all feel worse off for it is apparent that a modern equivalent would be very considerably more.

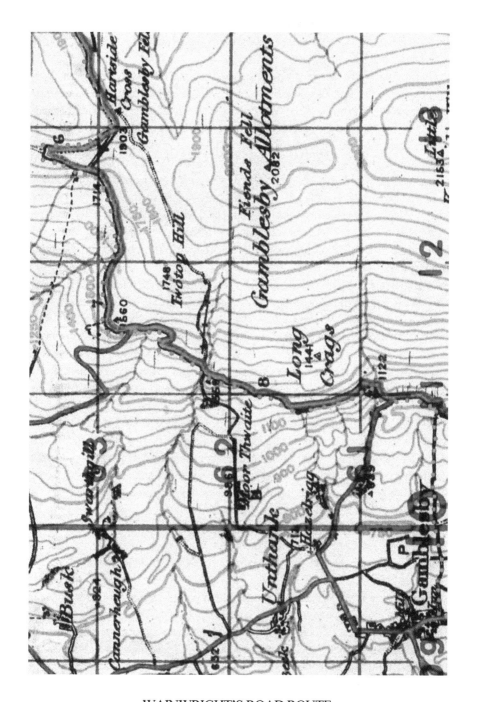

WAINWRIGHT'S ROAD ROUTE

AW awoke in his palatial surroundings extolling the virtues of his hosts and hoping that the young proprietors enjoyed success in their recent venture of having moved into the inn some months before.

He soon returned to his general malaise and commented on how this 'part of the journey proved to be the least interesting of all'. His entire account of the trek from Gamblesby to Brampton (just short of Appleby, he did not use the modern suffix of 'in Westmorland' as this was only added after the local government boundary changes of 1974) amounts to just one paragraph. The only highpoint was when, beyond Milburn, the hedgerows at the roadside reduced in height and he was able to see his beloved Lakeland fells.

He lamented that there 'was not a summit within view that had not been mine for a fleeting hour'. He referred to them as 'old friends', suggesting that even as early as 1938 he had visited a great many of the Lakeland hills. His first visit had been in 1930, when he experienced his road-to-Damascus transformation while atop Orrest Head. From his account on Day 9 of his Pennine journey it is abundantly clear that he would have much preferred to be with his 'old friends'.

We have looked closely at the social history associated with the places that we have visited during our eleven-day walk and occasionally have considered more global factors where they influenced AW's account, the obvious example being the underlying threat of European conflict. For the time being at least, back in 1938, the immediate threat of war was avoided. AW was happy about that fact as he was convinced he would have not made a good soldier. 1938 was also known for other events and this account has touched on one being the speed record for a steam locomotive, held by the Mallard in July 1938 which has never been surpassed.

Whereas this unbeaten record may seem very impressive, it has to be remembered that within a year the countries operating locomotives that might have challenged were immersed in war and speed records paled into insignificance. Once the war was over, the European countries generally proceeded with diesel-power and only Britain persisted with steam locomotion, and so it was that the record would never seriously be challenged because the technology had moved on.

AW's route during this part of his journey can only be surmised as a result of his brevity of narrative. He refers, in order, to Melmerby, Ousby, Skirwith, Blencarn and Milburn before rejoining with the route that he would have descended had he chosen to proceed over Cross Fell.

In passing these various Eden valley villages, AW paid no attention to the detail of each as he wearily trudged his way southwards. It is not the aim of this guide to attempt to identify a suitable modern way through the maze of hamlets for I assume that you will succeed in attaining the summits of Cross Fell and Great Dunn Fell. Leave these quiet settlements to be explored on a day out on four wheels. As delightful as they are, they do not compare with the alternative that AW himself would have aspired to.

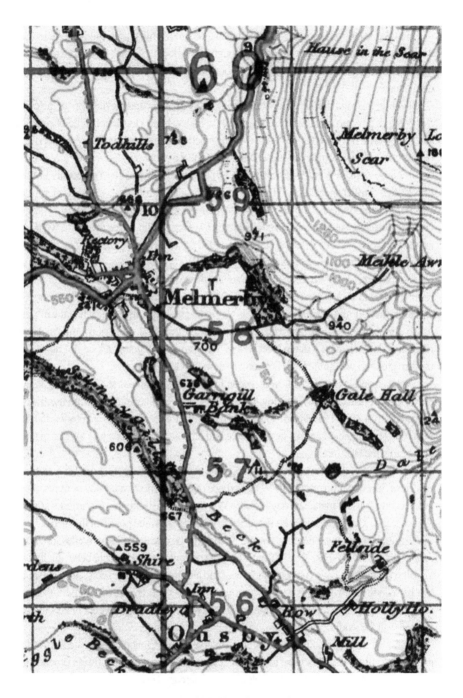

WAINWRIGHT'S ROAD ROUTE

In AW's continued southerly trek and his lament to the hills far to the west, he longed to be among them rather than 'trudging through this wilderness of green pasture and meadow'. He thought of their lofty heights and concluded that 'there was fruitful land; here was desolation.'

It was in this vein that he simply described Ousby as awful and the majority of the other dale villages as of no account. In adding insult to injury, black clouds appeared once again and by the time he arrived at the tea room in Appleby the rain was swilling the streets and only proceeded to become even more torrential as the day wore on.

In his account, AW refers to some detail of events elsewhere, more especially in relation to the conflict in Europe. The threat of impending hostilities was very clearly of concern to him but during the days of his escape from his 'old routine and irksome discipline' the threat appeared to have been diverted. However, within a year the world would be at war for six long years. The headlines from 1938 of storm clouds gathering over Europe were as a precursor to what was to follow.

On the more domestic front, anyone reading this who is of a particular age will fondly recall the Beano comic; first issued in July 1938 it must be assumed AW had not noticed, or that its humour did not appeal to him. It was issued weekly until 1941, when it was published fortnightly, sharing alternate weeks with its arch-rival the Dandy due to paper rationing. Unlike Britain's steam locomotion, the Beano is still going, although I doubt that modern children wait at the letter box for it to drop through the door.

Another classic British publication began life in 1938, with the first edition being issued on 1 October, just as AW was feeling relieved that Mr Chamberlain had saved us all from immediate war with Herr Hitler. Generally recognised as a pioneer in photo-journalism, Picture Post maintained an anti-fascist stance and amassed a vast library of images that are now within the BBC archives.

Turning away from the domestic market for comic book heroes, in the USA the first edition of Superman was issued in 1938. Perhaps one of the most well-known events of the year occurred just a matter of days after AW's return to Blackburn. In America, Orson Welles staged a very famous radio broadcast that was to show the power of the media.

On 30 October, the 'Mercury Theatre on the Air' broadcasted Orson Welles' dramatic adaptation of H. G. Wells' War of the Worlds. Its presentation had people believing that an invasion by Martians was currently underway and a state of panic gripped sectors of America. Its staging was without the usual commercial breaks and presented in a news-bulletin style with sudden interruptions and the outside broadcast suffering apparent breaks in connection with the studio.

Although the fictional nature of Welles' adaptation was made clear at the start of the programme, many listeners were tuned in to a popular Sunday evening music program on another channel, only changing channels after the Mercury Theatre had started.

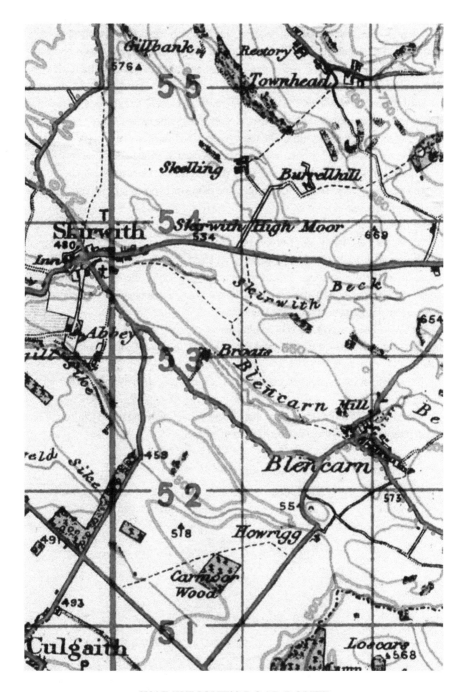

WAINWRIGHT'S ROAD ROUTE

Many listeners were fooled into believing that the Earth was actually being attacked by Martians and hundreds, possibly thousands, of people in New England, the base for the story, packed up cars and fled. There were stories of miscarriages and even death, although none was ever proved.

So was born the power of the radio. The newspapers were furious for they saw this new style of broadcasting as a cheap means of increasing the radio listener figures at the expense of the newspaper readers. The mass hysteria and the newspaper reportage of the ensuing anger was thought to have been over-exaggerated in an attempt by the newspapers to get people to turn against the newfangled wireless radio. Whatever the truth, the fact remains that the Welles' broadcast generated one of the most powerful responses that media has ever achieved.

So 1938 was a year to be reckoned with, not just because of the underlying fear of impending war but also for things of a more positive nature. Within a year, however, many of the events seen in 1938 would certainly not be repeated for many years, with society being placed in a state of suspended animation until 1945. Much of the exuberance of 1938 would not be seen until well after the end of the war years, for rationing and austerity measures were in place long after hostilities were ended.

In AW's closing words, he echoed his satisfaction, writing, 'The great thing was that there was not going to be a war. I would not have to be a soldier … life would be normal again.'

The very final words of his account were, 'I lit a cigarette, and idly watched the smoke curling upwards.'

There is nothing more I can add to that. Thank you for allowing me to join you; it has been a pleasure to revisit these wonderful days of escape.

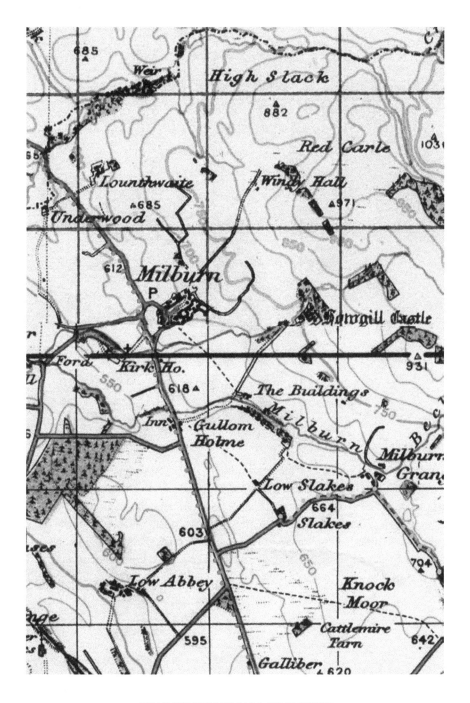

WAINWRIGHT'S ROAD ROUTE

ABOUT THE AUTHOR

Yorkshire-born author A Walker's writing centres around the earlier works of Alfred Wainwright, particularly his *Pennine Journey*, which he had undertaken in 1938. Walker retraced the route and found it became the inspiration for *Back to the Wall*, a personal reflection that uses the walk as a microcosm of life's journey. Walker's interpretation of his 1998 trek takes the form of a rambling account that compares and contrasts with Wainwright's original book using his own views and opinions as the basis of a thought-provoking and amusing yarn.

CPSIA information can be obtained
at www.ICGtesting.com
Printed in the USA
BVHW060056090221
599641BV00008B/1340